Quilts
Around the Year

Classic Quilts & Projects
for Every Season

Linda Seward

Illustrations by Penny Brown

A Sterling/Museum Quilts Book
Sterling Publishing Co., Inc. New York

Library of Congress Cataloging-in-Publication Data

Seward, Linda
    Quilts around the year: classic quilts and projects for every month / Linda Seward.
        p.   cm.
    Includes index.
    ISBN 0-8069-0710-X
    1. Quilting – Patterns. 2. Quilted goods. I. Title.
    TT835.S4615 1994
    746.46 – dc20   93-49718
                                                                    CIP

A Sterling/Museum Quilts Book

Published by Sterling Publishing Company, Inc.
387 Park Avenue South, New York, N.Y. 10016
And by
Museum Quilts Publications
254-258 Goswell Road, London EC1V 7EB

Distributed in Canada by Sterling Publishing
c/o Canadian Manda Group, P.O. Box 920, Station U
Toronto, Ontario, Canada M8Z 5P9

Distributed in Australia by Capricorn Link (Australia) Pty Ltd.
P.O. Box 6651, Baulkham Hills, Business Centre, NSW 2153, Australia

Copyright © 1994 by Museum Quilts Publications

Text © Linda Seward 1994
Illustrations © Penny Brown 1994
Photographs © Museum Quilts Publications 1994

Design: Carole Thomas Design Associates, designer Gabrielle Markus
Photography: *Antique quilts,* Ray Daffurn of Visionbank
            Jacket, Claude Simon
            Quilts in settings, Colin Mills

Antique quilts from the Susan Jenkins Collection, London

The publishers have made every effort to ensure that all instructions given in this book are accurate and safe, but they cannot accept liability for any resulting injury, damage or loss to either person or property whether direct or consequential and howsoever arising. The author and publisher will be grateful for any information which will assist them in keeping future editions up to date.

10 9 8 6 6 6 5 4 3 2 1

Typeset by Carole Thomas Design Associates, London
Index compiled by Susan Bosanko
Origination by Dong-A Publishing & Printing Co., Ltd, Korea
Printed and bound in Korea

ISBN 0-8069-0710-X

To the memory of my grandmothers,
Mary Fett and Ellen Macho,
who introduced me to needlework.
With patience and pride, they shared all their considerable
skills with their little granddaughter,
who has turned into a needlewoman herself.
I wish they were here today.

And for my mother, Evelyn Rose Macho,
who taught me all the rest.

Ellen Macho, Evelyn Rose Macho and Mary Fett.
This photograph was taken in Garfield, New Jersey in 1947.

Spring

Spring Bouquet

Art Deco Fans

Love Apple

Summer

Sunflowers

Summer Berries

Cactus Basket

Autumn

Birds in the Air

Rose Wreath

Rainbow Schoolhouses

Winter

Evergreen

Double Irish Chain

Oak Leaf and Reel

Contents

Introduction

Quilts Around the Year provides a glorious collection of quilts and projects that you can make to celebrate the four seasons of the year. The twelve exquisite antique quilt designs will tempt you to create different decorative themes in your home as spring melts into summer, summer changes to autumn and autumn cools into winter. Make seasonal quilts and you'll have a wonderful excuse to change the look of the rooms in your home throughout the year.

Springtime quilts are bright, cheery and full of blossoms and promises. Summertime quilts feature an array of flowers and fruit. Autumn themes are celebrated in an enchanting Rainbow Schoolhouses quilt, a glorious Birds in the Air quilt and a delicate Rose Wreath appliqué. A patchwork Evergreen tree quilt captures the crisp feeling of the snows of winter, while a mellow Double Irish Chain worked in Christmas colors of red, green and white makes one dream of the scent of wood smoke from log fires and gaily wrapped presents.

Each antique quilt has been photographed in full-color and is accompanied by its own personal history and an evocative piece of poetry. An illustration of a single block of the quilt is included to make it easy to understand the step-by-step instructions that follow.

In addition, for those who do not wish to make a complete quilt, each design has been adapted to create a small project. From the twelve attractive projects, you can choose to make elaborate pieces such as a wall hanging, table centerpiece or tote bag, or something very quick and easy such as a pot holder or cushion cover. Study the photographs of the small projects to see how the old designs are interpreted in modern fabrics. You can create the look of an antique, such as the table centerpiece or lap quilt, or you can make contemporary-looking pieces such as the baby quilt or pot holders.

The quilts and projects are rated by level of quilting expertise. The designs labelled *Beginner* can be tackled by fledgling quilters, *Intermediate* patterns are for those with some competence, and *Advanced* designs are for experienced quilters who are not afraid of a challenge.

The instructions for each quilt include the size of a single block and of the entire quilt, a complete list of materials, and step-by-step instructions accompanied by clear, full-color illustrations. Full-size templates for all the patterns are given at the back of the book. Quilting patterns, are also given at the back of the book. There is a chapter on quiltmaking techniques to enable even an inexperienced quilter to make each design in the book.

The instructions for the projects based on the antique quilt designs include the size of a single block (where applicable) and of the entire project, a complete list of materials, and step-by-step instructions. Because the projects are simple to construct, there is generally only an Assembly Diagram to guide you. However, whenever a technique hasn't been covered in the quilt instructions, additional diagrams are provided.

HOW TO BEGIN

After you have chosen the quilt that you wish to make, read through the instructions and review the step-by-step illustrations to make sure that you are capable of constructing the design. There is no point in starting a quilt or project that you will not be able to finish. If you like a design and aren't sure whether you can tackle it, try making only one block which you can then use to create a pot holder, cushion cover or small quilt. Use scraps so that you don't invest a lot of money in fabric, and have fun testing the design. If you are pleased with the results, you can then proceed with confidence.

If you are making a quilt, the next step is to decide how big you want the quilt to be. Most of the quilts in this book would be suitable for a double-size bed. If you wish to alter the size of a quilt, adjust the pattern by making more or less blocks or by adding or taking away borders and sashing. If you change the size of the quilt, you must adjust the fabric yardage too.

Next, and most important, is your choice of fabric. Following is a discussion of fabric – how it is constructed, how to make your color and print selections, and how to use modern fabrics to create an antique appearance.   ◆

Heirloom Fabrics

Fabric, cloth, material, textile – these words describe the tools and inspiration for quilters the world over. Fabric is the most important element in quilt making. But it is not just the physical use of fabric that is so important to quilt makers – it is the influence derived from fabric: its color and texture, whether it is a solid or a print and the scale of the print itself. It would be safe to say that the majority of quilt makers reading these words have at one time or another been stimulated by a certain fabric that they couldn't live without, whether because of a haunting combination of colors, a quirky repeat design, or simply an initial impression that couldn't be forgotten. The basic response (and one that is all too familiar to quilters) is to buy the fabric in enormous quantities to guard against the day when it runs out, and then go on to use that fabric as the basis for a magnificent quilt or wall hanging. This almost visceral response to fabric is what unites quilters of all ages and nationalities – a universal language of color and cloth.

The successful outcome of a patchwork or appliqué design is totally dependent on your selection of fabric. But when faced with a large selection of fabrics in a shop or at a quilt show, how do you go about choosing fabrics that will work for your special project?

TYPE OF FABRIC

First decide how you are going to use your quilt. If it is to be hung on a wall, you need only think of the aesthetic values of the materials you choose. But if the quilt is going to be used on a bed, it will have to stand up to constant wear and fairly regular washing. In this case, it is important to make sure that all the fabrics are of a similar weight. If you work with different weights of fabric, over time the stronger fabrics may pull apart the weaker ones, particularly at the seams. Choose fabrics with a medium weave; loosely-woven fabrics have little strength and tightly-woven fabrics will be troublesome to quilt. Very sheer fabrics and stretchy materials are unsuitable for quiltmaking, and heavy textiles are difficult to sew and quilt. The fabrics that you choose for a bed quilt should have the same laundry requirements – silk and cotton sewn edge-to-edge may cause problems.

The safest choice for those making bed quilts or quilted projects is dress weight, 100% cotton fabric. This washes and wears well and is easy to sew and quilt, either by hand or machine. It also presses more crisply than polyester-cotton blends, making it easier to achieve precise corners. So if you have a bag of fabric scraps that you have been saving for years to make a special quilt, sort through it and gently but firmly remove those fabrics manufactured with man-made fibers (in other words, polyester), and all those remnants left over from making curtains and sofa covers. They will not be suitable for making a bed quilt.

FABRIC CONSTRUCTION

When working so closely with fabric, it is helpful to understand a little about the way fabric works, and how it is constructed. This information is essential for optimum positioning when cutting out the pieces comprising a quilt or quilted project.

A fabric is woven with threads that cross each other at right angles. The warp thread runs the length of the fabric, and the weft or woof runs crosswise. If these threads cross each other at exact right angles, the fabric is said to be on grain or on the straight grain. If the fabric is off grain, it will be slightly skewed, and will not have the strong properties of a fabric that is on grain. You might be able to coax your fabric back to being on the straight grain as follows. With the aid of a friend, hold the four corners of the fabric. Pull diagonally from corner to corner, first in one direction and then in the other. Iron the fabric carefully and study the intersection of the threads. If the threads are not perpendicular to one another, the fabric is still off-grain and you will have to decide whether or not to use it. As a general rule, small pieces cut slightly off grain will not adversely affect a finished quilt or project. It is important, however, that your sashing, borders and any large pieces are cut on the straight grain.

Selvages are the finished edges of fabric; these must be

trimmed off and discarded because the edges are woven more tightly than the rest of the fabric and will shrink differentially. If you are tempted to use the selvage edges, particularly since they do not fray, steel yourself and cut them off; they will not add to the quality of your finished quilt or project, and may spoil the look of the piece after it is washed.

The lengthwise grain or *warp* runs parallel to the selvages; it has little stretch and is very strong. The borders and sashing of a quilt should be strong – therefore, cut them with the longest edges on the lengthwise grain of the fabric.

The *weft* or crosswise grain runs perpendicular to the selvages and has a very slight stretch. You can cut your normal patchwork and appliqué pieces across the weft of the fabric, but always place the longest edge of each piece on the straight grain of the fabric.

A fabric has its maximum stretch when it is cut on the *bias*, which runs at a 45° angle to the selvages. Curved patchwork should always be cut with the curved areas on the bias of the fabric so that the pieces are easier to manipulate. Appliquéd vines and binding that must go around curved areas are cut on the bias so that they can be readily controlled; see pages 108-109 for instructions on how to do this. When you are cutting out triangles, one edge is usually on the bias. This can cause problems if the bias edge is along the outside edge of the block – always study the composition of a patchwork block to determine the best way to cut the pieces out.

CHOOSING COLORS

I have specified the colors of the fabrics that were used to make the quilts and projects in this book mainly for ease in identifying the colors in the photographs. In this way, you can study the quilt or project and choose whether or not to make substitutions. Do not allow the specific colors that are listed to sway your choices. The color scheme is entirely at your own discretion: feel free to copy the quilts in the photographs exactly, or make up your own color scheme. If you are going to choose your own colors, the best way is to find one fabric that you absolutely love, and then select other fabrics that work well with it.

For the scrap quilts featured in this book, I have described the *value* of the color as simply *light, medium, bright* or *dark* – it would have proved an impossible task to describe every fabric! Value is the lightness or darkness of a color; it is almost more important than actual color when you are making a quilt. Values will seem to change depending on the fabrics surrounding them; this is useful to remember if you are working with a limited number of colors and wish to make the same colors appear different throughout your patchwork. Try to use an assortment of light, medium and dark values when selecting fabrics for making a quilt or quilted project.

PRINTED FABRICS

Printed fabrics are used to construct most traditional-style patchwork and appliqué quilts. Small-scale prints can be an attractive alternative to solid fabrics; these will add a subtle texture to a design. Micro-dot fabrics are especially useful for adding a slight sparkle to a quilt without competing with the other prints you may be using.

The most prevalent printed fabrics have a medium-scale design, which can vary from tightly compacted patterns to widely-spaced examples. These will probably form the backbone of your fabric choices, but don't be fooled into thinking that a range of beautifully matching medium-scale

prints will make a masterpiece quilt. You must have distinct contrast, both in color value and in the scale of your prints.

For an interesting alternative, choose large-scale prints which can produce surprising and unexpected effects. If you cut patchwork pieces from different sections of a large-scale fabric, your 'palette' will automatically expand because it will seem as if you have used more than just one fabric.

CREATING AN ANTIQUE APPEARANCE

The old quilts shown in this book were assembled with cotton fabrics contemporary to the period in which they were made; the date for each quilt can be found on the page opposite its large photograph. Since using old fabrics is not an option for most quilters, we have two choices. We can construct quilts in up-to-date fabrics, thus making a statement about the textiles that are obtainable today; future historians studying our quilts will be able to recognize and categorize the 'period' fabrics of the 1990's just as we study the fabrics in old quilts. The pot holders on page 85 illustrate how an old design can look when made up in contemporary fabrics.

Alternatively, we can use modern fabrics, but endeavour to achieve the appearance of an antique quilt by incorporating some of the suggestions that follow:

Part of the charm of an antique quilt is its 'old' appearance – the faded colors and the soft feel of the fabrics. If you are making a quilt from modern fabrics and wish to achieve an

antique effect, look for fabrics with a cream, beige or ecru background, or any fabrics dyed in soft colors. Pre-wash your fabrics several times using a fabric softener to remove any crispness or sizing from the manufacturing process. Alternatively, if you wish to work with crisp fabrics while piecing or appliquéing, pre-wash the fabrics only once to remove excess dye (see page 104 for instructions on pre-washing), and construct the quilt top. Then wash the finished quilt top to soften it. However, you must be warned about the thousands of threads that will magically appear on the back should you use this option!

Tea-dying has been a very popular way of treating white fabrics or prints that contain white areas to create an aged effect. However, tea contains tannic acid which can weaken the fibers, making them vulnerable to early deterioration.

Following is an easy method for tea-dyeing; it will work best with 100% cotton fabrics. Be sure to make a test sample first. Soak the fabric in water while preparing the tea bath. Place six tea bags in a saucepan and boil for about ten minutes; remove the bags. Place the soaked fabric in the tea and boil for about fifteen minutes; add a half cup of white vinegar to the water and boil for an additional ten minutes to set the dye. Remove the fabric and rinse thoroughly before drying and ironing it.

Many fabric companies are now producing delightful textile ranges with an 'heirloom' look

Another approach is to leave a brightly colored fabric in the sun to bleach naturally to a more muted shade, although any exposure to direct sunlight will weaken the fibers of the fabric and make them likely to break down earlier than they might have done. However, controlled 'bleaching' can be used effectively to create an aged effect.

Many of the fabrics manufactured in the 1920's and 1930's were absolutely delightful, and today's quilt scholars are having an enjoyable task finding, studying and cataloguing these textiles. Modern fabric manufacturers have not been unaware of the appeal of these old prints, and many of them are now reproducing similar designs for today's quilters. If you study the fabrics on these pages, you will find that some modern fabrics cannot be distinguished from those manufactured more than one hundred years ago. The use of 'reproduction' fabrics in your quiltmaking will certainly result in a quilt that has an antique appearance.

Plaid, striped and geometric fabrics are other options that shouldn't be ignored; they were widely used in quilts of the past and have hardly changed over time. These fabrics can add a touch of interest and excitement to a quilt, particularly if the plaids and stripes do not always run in the same direction or are cut slightly off-grain.

Try some of the techniques suggested here and you may find that you have achieved the quirky, charming folk art quality of an antique quilt. ◆

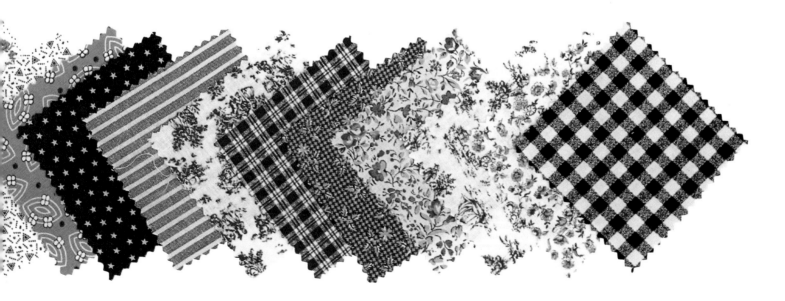

Spring

Spring Bouquet

The Passionate Shepherd to His Love, Christopher Marlowe (1564-1593)

Come live with me and be my love,
And we will all the pleasures prove,
That hills and valleys, dales and fields,
And all the craggy mountains yields.

There we will sit upon the rocks,
And see the shepherds feed their flocks,
By shallow rivers to whose falls
Melodious birds sing madrigals.

And I will make thee beds of roses
With a thousand fragrant posies,
A cap of flowers, and a kirtle
Embroidered all with leaves of myrtle;

The shepherds' swains shall dance and sing
For thy delight each May morning:
If these delights thy mind may move,
Then live with me and be my love.

This delightful appliquéd quilt evokes a sunny spring day perfumed with the scent of blossoms. It was made in the Midwestern United States during the 1930's from a published pattern. Each block is an exact replica of its neighbor, with no variation at all except for one (which may have been a deliberate mistake). However, the quirky vine in the border was probably the maker's own idea – it sports design elements from the blocks yet lacks the regularity of the rest of the piece. The plain blocks display a fine quilting design.

Spring Bouquet

ABILITY LEVEL: ADVANCED

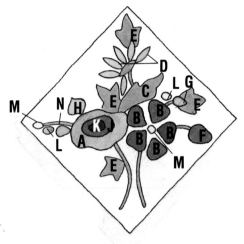

SIZE

Block: 12½ inches square;
12 blocks required
Finished quilt: 84 x 101¾ inches

MATERIALS

◆ 10 yards white fabric (includes fabric
for back of quilt and separate binding)
◆ 3¼ yards bright blue fabric — *green lt.*
◆ 2⅜ yards green fabric (includes *dark green —*
fabric for bias vine)
◆ ½ yard lavender fabric — *pink*
◆ ¼ yard pale pink fabric
◆ ¼ yard medium pink fabric *print*
◆ large scrap dark pink fabric — *pink*
◆ ⅜ yard yellow fabric ⟍ *¼ yd*
◆ large scrap yellow-orange fabric ⟋
◆ ⅜ yard medium blue fabric *print*
◆ 84½ x 102¼ inch piece of batting

CUTTING

Note: A ¼ inch seam allowance is
included in all measurements; templates
do not include a seam allowance. Full-
size templates can be found on pages
112-113.
Quilt back: 2 pieces, 42½ x 102¼
inches, white fabric.
Background squares: 12 O squares,
13 x 13 inches, white fabric; 6 O squares,
bright blue fabric.
Side P Triangles: Cut 2 squares from
the bright blue fabric, each 19 x 19

inches. Cut each square diagonally into 4
quarters to make 8 P triangles; use one
triangle as a pattern to cut 2 more
triangles for a total of 10.
Corner Q Triangles: Cut 2 squares from
the bright blue fabric, each 9⅞ x 9⅞
inches. Cut squares diagonally in half to
make 4 corner Q triangles.
Borders: 2 R strips 10½ x 54 inches,
white fabric; 2 S strips 10½ x 91¾
inches, white fabric; 2 T strips 5½ x 74
inches, bright blue fabric; 2 U strips
5½ x 102¼ inches, bright blue fabric.
Binding: Cut 9 strips across full width of
white fabric, each 1½ inches wide; stitch
strips together so binding measures
10½ yards long.
Bias binding for vine and stems:
From green fabric, cut one 44 inch
square and one 116 inch square.
Following the instructions for bias
binding on page 108, cut 1 inch wide bias

strips and sew together to measure
17½ yards long. Cut 12 lengths, each
18½ inches for the stems for the
appliquéd blocks. Cut one 10 yard length
for the vine on the border. Cut the
remaining bias stems as specified in the
chart in step 23.
Blocks: (Number of pieces for a single
block are in parenthesis.)

Pattern Piece	Number of Pieces	
A	(1)	12 pale pink
B	(5)	60 lavender
C	(1)	12 green
D	(1)	12 green
	(6)	72 medium blue
E	(4)	48 green
F	(1)	12 medium pink
G	(1)	12 yellow-orange
H	(1)	12 medium blue
J	(1)	12 medium pink
K	(1)	12 dark pink
L	(2)	24 yellow
M	(2)	24 yellow
N	(1)	12 yellow-orange

Borders:

B		60 lavender
D		8 green
		48 medium blue
E		36 green
F		8 medium pink
L		16 yellow
M		12 yellow

APPLIQUÉING A SPRING BOUQUET BLOCK

1 Trace the full-size pattern on pages 112–113, joining the pattern carefully along the dot/dash lines where it is split by the spine of the book. Keep this tracing whole and uncut for use in marking the white background **O** squares.

2 Make a separate template for each piece as directed on page 105. Use the templates to cut out the pieces for one block as directed in the cutting instructions.

3 Using a pencil and the complete tracing you made in step 1, mark the major placement lines on the right side of one white **O** square: mark the edges of the **A, B, C** and green **D** pieces as shown; also mark 6 lines to indicate the positions of the stems.

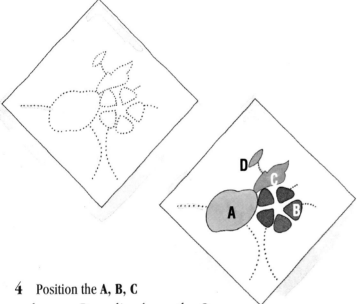

4 Position the **A, B, C** and green **D** appliqués on the **O** square over the pencil lines marked in step 3; pin in place.

5 From the 18½ inch length of green bias strip you previously prepared, cut 6 stems following the measurements given in the chart above right; a ¼ inch allowance is included in each measurement. Pin the stems in their correct position on the background square. Where the stems touch an appliqué, tuck the raw end of the stem ¼ inch beneath the appliqué. Finish the other end of the stem by turning the raw edge under ¼ inch. Steam-press each strip gently until it follows the

contours of the lines marked on the background square. When you are satisfied with the curves, hand-baste the stems in place down the middle of each.

Stem	Length
1	3¼ inches
2	5¾ inches
3	5¼ inches
4	1½ inches
5	1 inch
6	1¾ inches

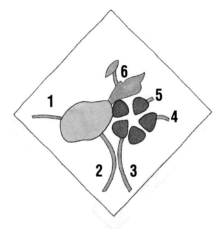

6 Arrange the blue **D** petals around the green **D** appliqué as shown. Pin in place. Next, arrange the **E** leaves on the background square, tucking one beneath a blue **D** petal as shown. Position the **F** bud over the end of its stem. Place the **G** bud over the join of the **E** leaf to its stem. Tuck the base of the **H** petal beneath **A**. Appliqué these pieces and the stems to the background square using matching thread; see how to appliqué on pages 107–108. Remove all pins and basting.

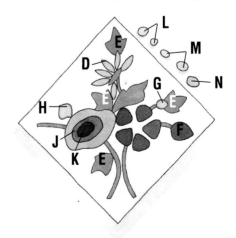

7 Position the **J** and **K** pieces on top of **A** as shown in the artwork for step 6 on the previous page. Appliqué in place.

8 Following the block plan on page 16, position the remaining **L, M** and **N** pieces on the background square. Appliqué each piece in place using matching thread.

9 Construct 11 more Spring Bouquet blocks.

ASSEMBLY

10 Following the **Quilt Plan** and working on a large flat surface, arrange the appliquéd blocks on point with the blue **O** squares to form a checkerboard pattern.

11 Position the **P** border triangles along the 4 side edges and position the **Q** corner triangles in the 4 corners of the quilt.

12 Sew the appliquéd and plain blocks together in diagonal rows; sew a **P** or **Q** triangle to each end of each row.

13 Join the diagonal rows together, starting with the long middle rows, and working outward to the corners, matching seams carefully. Sew the remaining 2 **Q** pieces to the corners to complete the middle of the quilt top.

BORDERS

14 Stitch an **R** border to the top and bottom edges of the pieced and appliquéd top. Stitch an **S** border to the side edges.

15 Stitch a **T** border to the top and bottom edges of the pieced and appliquéd top. Stitch a **U** border to each side edge to complete the quilt top.

16 You may wish to zigzag-stitch the edges of the **T** and **U** border pieces to prevent them from fraying while you work on the appliquéd border.

17 First study the diagrams **Border R** and **Border S** to see how the border design works. On each border, the bias vine has 5 curves; these curves are deep on the **R** border and shallow on the **S** border. Using 2 pins for each, divide the **R** and **S** borders evenly into 3 sections.

18 Take the green bias strip vine you have previously prepared and begin in the top left corner of the quilt where the first **E** leaf will be placed. Pin the end of the vine in place, then following the **Border R** diagram, work to the right across the top **R** border, making 5 curves as shown and matching up curves 2 and 4 with the pin marks you measured in step 17. This process will take some time, but with gentle steam-pressing and patience it will work. When you are satisfied with the vine, baste it in place.

QUILT PLAN

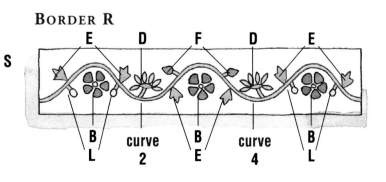

BORDER R

19 When you reach the top right corner, make a gentle loop with the vine as shown in the **Quilt Plan.** Steam-press it into position then, when you are satisfied, baste it in place.

20 Next, following the **Quilt Plan** and the **Border S** diagram, position the vine along the right side of the quilt, making 5 gentle curves as shown and matching up curves 2 and 4 with the pin marks measured in step 17. Steam-press, then baste.

21 When you reach the bottom right corner, make a gentle loop with the vine as you did in step 19. Steam-press, then baste.

22 Repeat steps 18-21 to position and baste the vine to the remaining 2 border pieces. When the end of the vine meets the beginning, trim away any excess vine, leaving ¹/₄ inch for turning under. Lap one end over the other, folding the raw edge under and baste in place.

23 Next, following the chart below, cut the stem pieces for the border (a ¹/₄ inch allowance is included).

Stem Piece	Length	Number
D stems	2¹/₄ inches	8
F stems	1¹/₄ inches	8
L stems	1 inches	16

24 Prepare the remaining border pieces for appliqué. Following the border diagrams, arrange the appliqués and stem pieces along the vine, tucking the ends of the stems beneath the vine and overlapping the other end of each stem with its respective appliqué. Pin or baste the pieces in place, then appliqué all the border pieces in place using matching thread.

25 To construct the quilt back, sew the long edges of the 2 fabric pieces together. Press the seam allowance to one side.

FINISHING

26 Assemble the quilt as directed on page 109.

27 Outline-quilt the pieces on the appliquéd blocks.

28 See page 114 for the full-size quilting patterns. Complete the quarter-pattern for the design for the plain blocks; make a template and transfer to the center of each of the blue **O** squares.

29 Make a template for the border design and transfer to the **T** and **U** pieces, repeating the geometric portion of the design across the pieces and adjusting it to fit between the flowers in the corners. Allow a petal of each flower to overlap the white borders in each of the corners as shown. Also, transfer a flower to the corners of the white borders inside the loop of the vine as shown on the **Quilt Plan.** Quilt all the marked designs.

30 Bind the quilt with a separate binding as directed on pages 110-111.

BORDER S

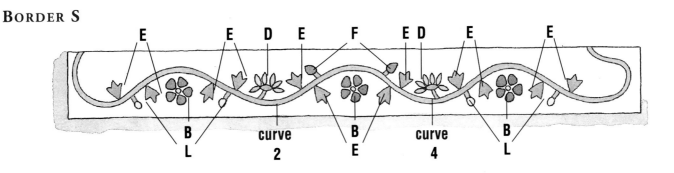

Art Deco Fans

Songs sung in Arden, William Shakespeare (1564-1616)

It was a lover and his lass,
With a hey, and a ho, and a hey nonino,
That o'er the green corn-field did pass,
In spring time, the only pretty ring time,
When birds do sing, hey ding a ding, ding;
Sweet lovers love the spring.

It is hard to believe that this quilt was made during America's Depression era. Perhaps it provided a welcome spot of color and cheer at a time when it was needed. The careful placement of the red patches creates a sense of movement and vitality, while the bright yellow and green fabrics seem to shout that spring (and better times) are just around the corner. The quilt contains a wonderful variety of 1930's fabrics; in her search for bright colors, the quilt maker even used corduroy to achieve just the right effect.

Art Deco Fans

ABILITY **L**EVEL: **I**NTERMEDIATE/**A**DVANCED

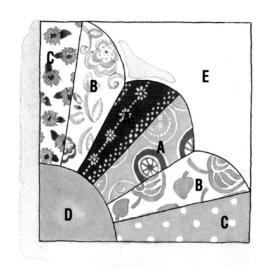

SIZE

Block: 7¹/₂ inches square;
98 blocks required
Finished quilt: 75¹/₂ x 86¹/₄ inches

MATERIALS

Note: This is a scrap quilt, where the maker used the fabrics she had on hand to create each block – no two blocks are the same. The yardages that are given below assume that you will be using the same fabric for the background **E** pieces (light), the **D** fan bases (dark) and three fabrics for the fan pieces **A, B** and **C** (medium, medium-bright and bright) throughout the entire quilt. If you wish to make a quilt that resembles the antique example shown here, choose an assortment of scrap fabrics for the fan pieces, but use the same fabric throughout for all the fan bases. If you are making a scrap quilt, refer to the yardages below to give yourself a general idea of how much fabric you will need to

make the quilt.

◆ 7¹/₂ yards light fabric (includes fabric for back of quilt and separate binding)
◆ ³/₄ yard dark fabric
◆ 2 yards medium fabric
◆ 2 yards medium-bright fabric
◆ 2 yards bright fabric
◆ ⁷/₈ yard coordinating fabric for border triangles
◆ 76 x 86³/₄ inch piece of batting

CUTTING

Note: A ¹/₄ inch seam allowance is included in all measurements; templates do not include a seam allowance. Full-size templates can be found on page 123.
Quilt back: 2 pieces, 38¹/₄ x 86³/₄ inches, light fabric
Side F Triangles: Cut 6 squares from the coordinating fabric, each 12 x 12

inches. Cut each square diagonally into 4 quarters to make 24 triangles ; use one triangle as a pattern to cut 2 additional triangles for a total of 26 **F** triangles.
Corner G Triangles: Cut 2 squares from the coordinating fabric, each 6³/₈ x 6³/₈ inches. Cut each square diagonally in half to make 4 corner **G** triangles.
Binding: Cut 8 strips across the full width of the light fabric, each 1¹/₂ inches wide; stitch strips together so binding measures 9 yards long.
Blocks: (Number of pieces for a single block are in parenthesis.)

Pattern Piece	Number of Pieces	
A	(1)	98 medium
A(R)	(1)	98 bright
B	(1)	98 medium-bright
B(R)	(1)	98 medium-bright
C	(1)	98 bright
C(R)	(1)	98 medium
D	(1)	98 dark
E	(1)	98 light

PIECING AN ART DECO FAN BLOCK

1 Sew each **A** to a reversed **A**.

2 Sew **B** to **C**, leaving the top ¼ inch unsewn (indicated by dots on the illustration). Then sew a reversed **B** to a reversed **C** in the same manner.

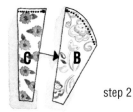

step 1

3 Sew the **B** edge of each B-C piece to A-A.

4 Sew **D** to the lower curved edge of the fan; see page 107 for instructions on how to sew curves.

step 2

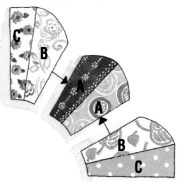

5 Mark the placement lines on the **E** template onto the right side of **E**. To prepare the fan for appliqué, fold and press the curved edges of the **A** and **B** pieces ¼ inch to the wrong side; the seam allowance for **C** will extend beyond the other pieces. Position the fan over **E**, matching up the edges of the fan with the marked lines on **E**. Pin, then appliqué in place.

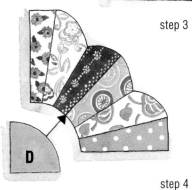

step 3

step 4

6 Construct 97 more Art Deco Fan blocks.

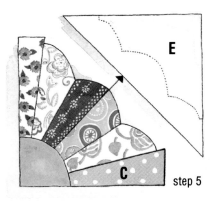

step 5

ASSEMBLY AND FINISHING

7 Following the **Quilt Plan**, arrange the patchwork blocks on point to create 15 horizontal rows, alternating 7 blocks in one row with 6 blocks in the adjacent row.

8 Position the **F** triangles along the side edges of the quilt. Position the **G** corner triangles in the 4 corners of the quilt.

9 Sew the patchwork blocks together in diagonal rows, making sure to sew an **F** or **G** triangle to each end of each row.

10 Join the diagonal rows, starting with the long middle rows, and working outward to the corners. Sew the remaining 2 **G** corner pieces to the corners to complete the quilt top.

11 To construct the quilt back, sew the long edges of the 2 fabric pieces together. Press the seam allowance to one side.

12 Assemble the quilt as directed on page 109.

13 Follow the lines on the templates to quilt the blocks.

14 Make a template for the *fleur-de-lis* pattern on page 123. Transfer to the **F** and **G** border triangles; quilt.

15 Bind the quilt with a separate binding; see pages 110-111.

QUILT PLAN

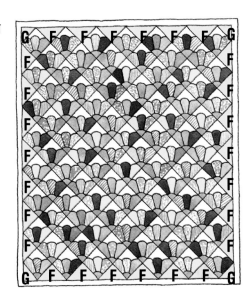

Love Apple

A Birthday, Christina Rossetti (1830-1894)

My heart is like a singing bird
Whose nest is in a watered shoot:
My heart is like an apple tree
Whose boughs are bent with thickset fruit;
My heart is like a rainbow shell
That paddles in a halcyon sea;
My heart is gladder than all these
Because my love is come to me...

The pleasing regularity of the appliquéd motifs is enhanced by the intricate patchwork border. This is a typical example of the many beautiful quilts that were made to honor the *'Love Apple'* – what we now call the tomato. It was then much admired by gardeners, but the fruit was considered to be inedible. The quilt was made in Pennsylvania around 1880.

Love Apple
ABILITY LEVEL: ADVANCED

SIZE
Block: 22 inches square;
12 blocks required
Finished quilt: 73 x 95 inches

MATERIALS
◆ 13 yards white fabric (includes fabric for back of quilt)
Note: If you use 54 inch wide fabric you will need 9 yards
◆ 2 yards red fabric
◆ 3¼ yards green fabric
◆ 1¾ yards yellow fabric
◆ ⅜ yard coordinating fabric for binding
◆ 73½ x 95½ inch piece of batting

CUTTING
Note: A ¼ inch seam allowance is included in all measurements; templates do not include a seam allowance. Full-size templates can be found on page 122.

Quilt back: 2 pieces, 37 x 95½ inches, white fabric.

Background squares: 12 squares, each 22½ x 22½ inches square, white fabric.

Binding: Cut 8 strips across the full width of the coordinating fabric, each 1½ inches wide; stitch the strips together so that the binding measures 9½ yards long.

Blocks: (Number of pieces for a single block are in parenthesis.)

Pattern Pieces	Number of Pieces	
A	(1)	12 red
B	(2)	24 green
C	(8)	96 red
D	(8)	96 yellow
E	(4)	48 green
E(R)	(4)	48 green
F	(8)	96 green
G	(1)	12 yellow
Side Borders:		
H		44 yellow
		84 red
J		88 green
K		8 green
Top/Bottom Borders:		
H		36 yellow
		34 red
J		72 green
K		8 green

PIECING A LOVE APPLE BLOCK
1 First prepare a base for the appliqués. Fold a background square in half horizontally and vertically; press carefully. Open out the block and hand-baste a row of stitches along each of the folds. Press the base to remove the folds. Then, measure 7½ inches away from the center point on one of the basted lines and mark 2 **X's** for the placement of the **B** appliqués.

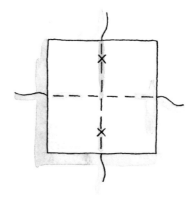

2 Trace the full-size patterns for the appliqués and make a separate template for each piece as directed on page 105. Use the templates to cut out the pieces for one block as directed in the cutting instructions (cut the number of pieces in parenthesis). Prepare the pieces for appliqué as directed on page 107. You needn't turn under the inner curved edges of the **C**, **D** and **E** pieces as these areas will be tucked beneath adjacent appliqués; study the block plan on the facing page.

3 Position the **A** flower in the middle of the background square, centered exactly over the place where the basting lines cross. Baste, then appliqué in place using matching thread. See pages 107-108 for instructions on how to appliqué.

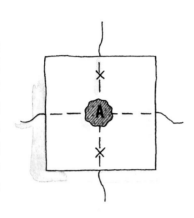

4 Position the **B** appliqués on the background square above and below the **A** flower, with the middle of each B centered over one of the X's you marked in step 1. Baste the **B** pieces in place along the middle of each appliqué. Remove the basting stitches from the base.

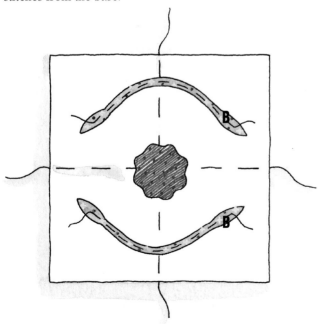

5 Arrange the red **C** petals on each side of the tips of the **B** appliqués, tucking the inner curved edges of **C** beneath **B**. Pin in place.

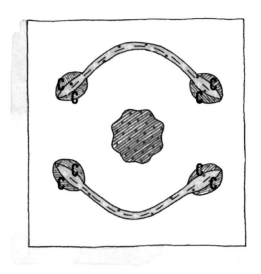

6 Arrange the **D** appliqués on each side of the **C** pieces, tucking the inner curved edges of **D** beneath **C** as shown. Pin in place.

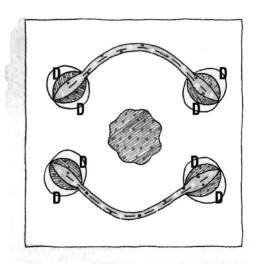

7 Next, arrange the **E** leaves on each side of each **D**, tucking the inner curved edges of **E** beneath **D**. Appliqué the **C**, **D** and **E** pieces in place using matching thread.

8 Position the **F** leaves on each side of the **B** stems, angling the leaves as shown; baste. Appliqué the **F** and **B** pieces in place using matching thread. Remove the basting stitches from each **B**. Position **G** in the middle of the **A** flower; appliqué in place.

9 Construct 11 more Love Apple blocks in the same manner.

BORDER

10 To construct the patchwork border for one side edge of the quilt, begin by sewing a red **H** to opposite sides of a yellow **H**. Repeat until you have 20 **H-H-H** strips.

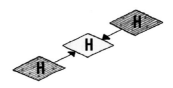

11 Sew a **J** triangle to the red **H** on each side of each strip as shown.

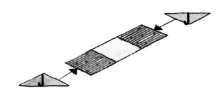

12 Next construct the edging triangles (to be sewn to each end of each strip): sew a red **H** to a yellow **H**, making two **H-H** pairs. Sew a **J** triangle to the red **H** and a **K** triangle to the yellow **H**. Then, sew a **J** to a **K** piece as shown; sew **J-K** to the **K-H-H-J** strip to make one edging triangle. Make another edging triangle in the same manner for the opposite end of the border.

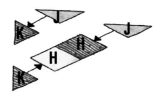

13 Sew the patchwork strips together, aligning the yellow **H** diamonds as shown. Then sew an edging triangle to each end of the patchwork strip. Construct another side border strip in the same manner.

14 To construct the top border, begin by sewing a red **H** to opposite sides of a yellow **H** as you did in step 10. Repeat until you have 17 **H-H-H** strips.

15 Sew a **J** triangle to the red **H** on each side of each strip as you did in step 11.

16 Construct 2 edging triangles as you did in step 12.

17 Sew the 17 **J-H-H-H-J** strips together, aligning the yellow **H** diamonds as you did in step 13. Sew an edging triangle to each end of the strip. Construct the bottom border strip in the same manner.

ASSEMBLY

18 Following the **Quilt Plan** and working on a large flat surface, arrange the patchwork blocks in 4 horizontal rows with 3 blocks in each row. Make sure the blocks are all facing in the same direction.

QUILT PLAN

19 Stitch the blocks together in rows.

20 Stitch the rows together, matching seams carefully at the intersections.

21 Stitch a patchwork side border to each long side edge of the quilt top.

22 Fold the top border strip in half lengthwise to find the middle; match to the center of the middle appliquéd block along the top edge of the quilt; pin together. Pin the remainder of the border to the quilt top; there will be 1/2 inch excess at each side edge. Stitch the border to the quilt, then trim off the excess patchwork at each end. Repeat for the bottom border strip.

23 To construct the quilt back, sew the long edges of the two fabric pieces together. Press the seam allowance to one side.

24 Assemble the quilt top, batting and back as directed on page 109.

FINISHING

25 Outline-quilt the love apple, stem and leaf appliqués following the lines on the templates.

26 Quilt the white background in a cross-hatch design. Using a pencil or chalk, draw a straight diagonal line connecting the opposite corners of the quilt. Repeat this line in the other direction so that you have drawn an X across the quilt. (Do not draw the X on top of the appliqués, just between them on the white background.) Quilt along these marked lines, then work parallel lines of quilting to the left and right of these lines, spacing the lines 2 inches apart. Where the quilting lines cross, they will create a cross-hatch pattern.

27 Bind the quilt with a separate binding as directed on pages 110-111.

Summer

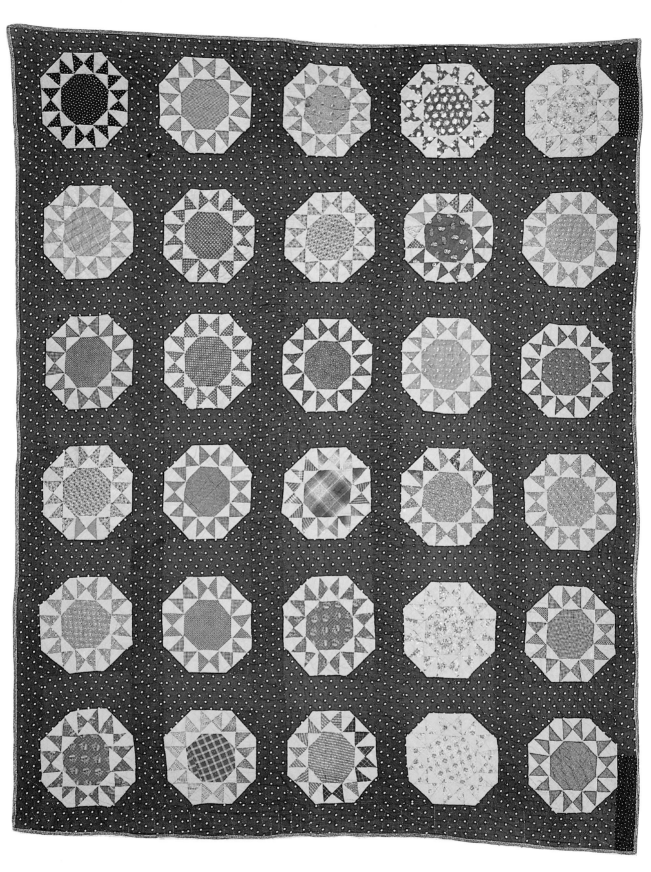

Sunflowers

Ah! Sun-Flower, William Blake (1757-1827)

Ah Sun-flower! weary of time,
Who countest the steps of the Sun:
Seeking after that sweet golden clime,
Where the travellers journey is done.

Where the Youth pined away with desire,
And the pale Virgin shrouded in snow:
Arise from their graves and aspire,
Where my Sun-flower wishes to go.

This North Carolina quilt maker knew exactly what she was doing when she chose the navy polka-dot background fabric – it makes the patchwork sunflowers appear to glow in the warmth of a starry summer night. The sunflower centers and petals are a wonderful catalog of the brown fabrics available at the turn of the century – the time when this quilt was made.

Sunflowers

ABILITY LEVEL: INTERMEDIATE

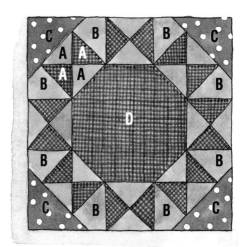

SIZE

Block: 9¹/₂ inches square;
30 blocks required
Finished quilt: 66¹/₂ x 79¹/₂ inches

MATERIALS

◆ 3¹/₄ yards gold fabric (includes fabric
for binding)
◆ 2⁵/₈ yards brown fabric
◆ 6³/₄ yards blue polka dot fabric
(includes fabric for back of quilt)
◆ 67 x 80 inch piece of batting

CUTTING

Note: A ¹/₄ inch seam allowance is
included in all measurements; templates
do not include a seam allowance. Full-
size templates can be found on page 119.
Quilt back: 2 pieces, 40¹/₄ x 67 inches,
blue dot fabric.
Sashing: 24 **E** strips, 4 x 10 inches; 5 **F**

strips, 4 x 62 inches, blue dot fabric.
Borders: 2 **G** strips 3 x 62 inches, blue
dot fabric; 2 **H** strips 3 x 80 inches, blue
dot fabric.
Binding: Cut 7 strips across the full
width of the gold fabric, each 1¹/₂ inches
wide; stitch strips together so binding
measures 8¹/₄ yards long.
Blocks: (Number of pieces for a single
block are in parenthesis.)

Pattern Piece	Number of Pieces	
A	(16)	480 gold
	(16)	480 brown
B	(8)	240 gold
C	(4)	120 blue dot
D	(1)	30 brown

— ● ◆ ● —

PIECING A SUNFLOWER BLOCK

1 Sew a brown **A** to a gold **A**
to form a pieced triangle with
the brown triangle on the left
and the gold triangle on the
right. Construct a total of 10 **A-
A** triangles in this manner.

2 Sew 2 pairs of **A-A** triangles
together to form a pieced
square. Repeat 3 more times
for a total of 4 **A-A** squares. (2
A-A triangles are left over for
use in Step 8.)

3 Sew the long
edges of 2 **B**'s to the
brown patches of an
A-A square. Repeat
3 more times for a
total of 4 **B-A-B**
sections; set 2
sections aside for
use in Step 8.

4 Sew 4 gold **A**'s
to opposite corners
of the **D** octagon,
forming a square.

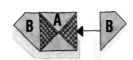

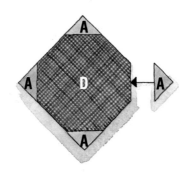

5 Sew a brown **A** triangle to the long edges of 2 **B-A-B** strips, then sew to opposite sides of the **A-D** square.

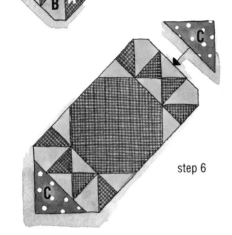

step 5

6 Sew a **C** triangle to opposite edges of the patchwork.

7 Sew a gold **A** to a brown **A** to form a pieced triangle with the gold triangle on the left and the brown triangle on the right. Repeat to make a second **A-A** triangle in the same manner.

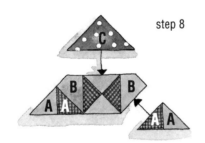

step 6

step 7

step 8

8 Sew the **A-A** triangles made in Step 7 to the left edge of the remaining 2 **B-A-B** sections. Sew the **A-A** triangles made in Step 2 to the right edge of the 2 **B-A-B** sections. Sew a **C** to the top.

9 Sew the large pieced triangles to the patchwork.

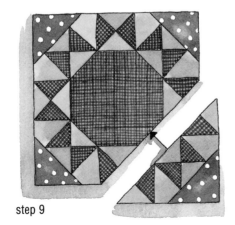

step 9

10 Construct 29 more Sunflower blocks in the same manner.

ASSEMBLY

11 Following the **Quilt Plan**, arrange the blocks in 6 horizontal rows with 5 blocks in each row. Position **E** and **F** sashing strips between the blocks.

12 Stitch the blocks to the **E** sashing strips. Stitch the horizontal rows to each side of each **F** strip.

13 Sew a **G** border to the top and bottom edges. Sew an **H** border strip to each side edge of the patchwork.

14 To construct the quilt back, sew the long edges of the 2 fabric pieces together. Press the seam allowance to one side.

15 Assemble the quilt as directed on page 109.

FINISHING

16 Quilt the entire surface of the quilt in a wave pattern as shown in the Quilting Diagram on page 118.

17 Bind the quilt as directed on pages 110-111.

QUILT PLAN

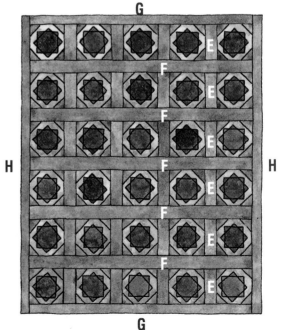

Summer Berries

Sonnet, William Shakespeare (1564-1616)

Shall I compare thee to a summer's day?
Thou art more lovely and more temperate:
Rough winds do shake the darling buds of May,
And summer's lease hath all too short a date:
Sometime too hot the eye of heaven shines,
And often is his gold complexion dimmed;
And every fair from fair sometime declines,
By chance, or nature's changing course untrimmed;
But thy eternal summer shall not fade,
Nor lose possession of that fair thou owest,
Nor shall Death brag thou wanderest in his shade,
When in eternal lines to time thou growest;
  So long as men can breathe, or eyes can see,
  So long lives this, and this gives life to thee.

Although this impressive 1860's piece was probably a 'best quilt' (one made only for use on very special occasions), it is not a traditional 'best' quilt – it retains a sense of lightness and fun. Perhaps the oddly shaped berry trees on the borders and the flash of gold at the tip of each cluster save it from being too formal.

Summer Berries

ABILITY LEVEL: ADVANCED

SIZE
Block: 17 inches square;
12 blocks required
Finished quilt: 72 x 78½ inches

MATERIALS
◆ 9¾ yards cream fabric (includes fabric for back of quilt, borders and self-binding)
◆ 1¼ yards red fabric
◆ 2½ yards green fabric
◆ ¼ yard yellow fabric
◆ 72½ x 79 inch piece of batting

TEMPLATES
C1: 1¾ inch diameter circle (includes seam allowance; use this template to cut the fabric berries)
C2: 1¼ inch diameter circle (does not include seam allowance; make about 50 templates out of thin cardboard)

CUTTING
Note: A ¼ inch seam allowance is included in all measurements; templates do not include a seam allowance. Full-size templates can be found on page 121.
Background Squares: 12 squares, each 17½ x 17½ inches, cream fabric.
Quilt back: 2 pieces, 37½ x 81 inches, cream fabric (includes extra 2 inches for self-binding).
Borders: From cream fabric, cut one **E** strip, 11 x 51½ inches; 2 **F** strips 28 x 11 x 79 inches.

B Stems: From green fabric, cut 4 strips across full width of fabric, each 1¼ inches wide; cut strips into 3½ inch lengths for a total of 48 **B** stems.
Blocks: (Number of pieces for a single block are in parenthesis.)

Pattern Piece	Number of Pieces	
A	(1)	12 red
B	(4)	48 green
C1	(5)	60 yellow
	(24)	288 green
	(32)	384 red
D	(4)	48 green
D (R)	(4)	48 green
Border:		
C1		23 yellow
		138 green
		184 red
D		23 green
D (R)		23 green
G		23 green

• ◆ •

APPLIQUÉING A SUMMER BERRIES BLOCK
1 First prepare a base for the appliqués. Fold a background square in half diagonally first in one direction and then the other; press carefully. Open out the block and hand-baste a row of stitches along each of the diagonal folds. Press the base to remove the folds.

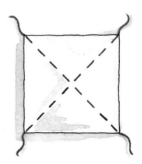

2 Prepare an **A** flower for appliqué as directed on page 107. Place in the exact middle of the base and hand-baste in place.

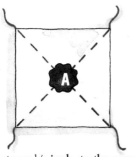

3 Fold the long raw edges of 4 **B** stems ¼ inch to the wrong side and press carefully. Place the middle of each stem over a hand-basted diagonal line, tucking the end of each stem ¼ inch under the edge of the **A** flower. Baste in place.

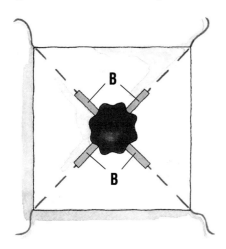

4 Prepare 4 yellow berries, 24 green berries and 32 red berries for appliqué as follows. Work a row of basting stitches close to the edge of a fabric circle. Place the cardboard **C2** template in the middle of the fabric circle.

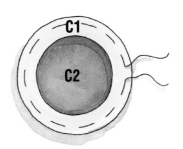

5 Gently pull the basting stitches to gather the edge of the fabric circle around the **C2** template. Make a few backstitches to secure the end of the thread. Press the gathered circle gently so that there are no puckers or pleats on the right side. Then,

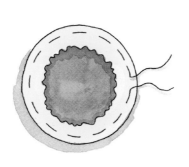

carefully pop the cardboard template out of the fabric circle without distorting the pressed shape. The berry is ready to appliqué to the fabric.

6 Measure 1¼ inches in from each edge of each corner and mark a dot. Center a yellow berry over each dot and pin in place.

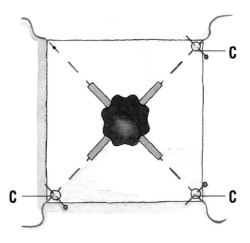

7 Arrange 5 red berries in a straight row across the top of each **B** stem, covering the end of the stem with the central berry. Pin the berries in place.

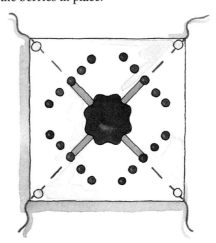

8 Arrange the remainder of the berries in rows, staggering the berries to make a neat triangular shape. Place 4 green berries in the second row, 3 red berries in the third row, and 2 green berries in the fourth row. These should fit neatly beneath the yellow berry already pinned in each corner.

9 When you are satisfied with the placement, baste the berries to the base, then appliqué the berries in place using matching thread as directed on page 108.

10 Prepare 4 **D** and 4 reversed **D** leaves for appliqué as directed on pages 107-108. Position a leaf and its reverse on each side of each stem as shown. When you are satisfied with the position of the leaves, appliqué the leaves and stems in place using matching thread.

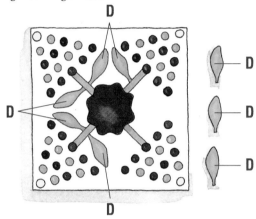

11 Appliqué the flower to the base using red thread. Place the remaining yellow berry in the exact middle of the flower and appliqué it in place using yellow thread. If you wish, you can emphasize this berry with high-relief appliqué as directed on the facing page.

12 Construct 11 more Summer Berries blocks in the same manner.

ASSEMBLY

13 Following the Quilt Plan (as shown above right) and working on a large flat surface, arrange the appliquéd blocks in 4 horizontal rows with 3 blocks in each row. Stitch the blocks together in horizontal rows, then stitch the rows together, matching seams carefully at the intersections.

14 Sew the **E** border strip to the bottom of the quilt top.

15 Sew the **F** border strips to the side edges of the quilt top.

QUILT PLAN

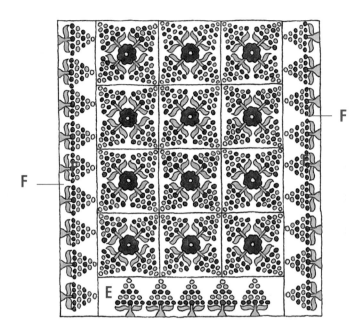

APPLIQUÉD BORDER

16 To construct the appliquéd border, first measure and mark the following points along the bottom **E** border strip, measuring the distances along the seam from left to right as shown in the diagram below. (Note that these points bisect the appliquéd blocks at the midpoints and the seams.)

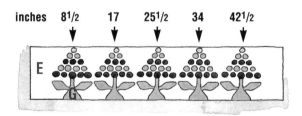

17 Prepare 5 yellow berries, 30 green berries and 40 red berries for appliqué as you did for the blocks. Also prepare 10 leaves. Turn only the curved side edges of 5 **G** stems to the wrong side to prepare them for appliqué; you need not turn under the top and bottom edges.

18 Place a yellow berry at each of the marked points so that the top edge of the berry just touches the seamline. Pin in place.

19 Arrange the remainder of the berries in 4 rows beneath each yellow berry, making a neat triangular shape as follows. Place 2 green berries in the second row, 3 red berries in the third row, 4 green berries in the fourth row and 5 red berries in the fifth row.

20 Position a **G** stem beneath each of the middle berries in the fifth row, tucking the top raw edge of **G** beneath the berry; the bottom raw edge of **G** should line up with the raw edge of the quilt top.

21 Place a **D** leaf and its reverse on each side of each **G** stem, tucking the raw ends beneath the **G** stems.

22 When you are satisfied with the placement of the pieces, appliqué them to the border using matching thread.

23 Next, appliqué the side border pieces. Measure and mark the following points along each of the **F** border strips (as shown below), measuring the distances along the seam from the top to the bottom of the quilt (the top edge is the one without a border). Note that these points are marked every 8$\frac{1}{2}$ inches. There will be a 6$\frac{1}{2}$ inch space left at the bottom of the quilt.

24 Prepare 18 yellow berries, 108 green berries and 144 red berries for appliqué as you did for the blocks. Also prepare 36 leaves and 18 **G** stems for appliqué.

25 Place a yellow berry at each of the marked points so that the top edge of the berry just touches the seamline. Pin in place.

26 Arrange the remaining appliqués as you did for the bottom border. Appliqué in place using matching thread.

FINISHING

27 For the quilt back, sew the long edges of the 2 fabric pieces together. Press the seam allowance to one side.

28 Assemble the quilt top, batting and back as directed on page 109, centering the top and batting over the back which will be larger all around.

29 Outline-quilt the berries, leaves and stems.

30 Quilt the background fabric in a cross-hatched grid. First, quilt straight lines in one diagonal direction, spaced 1 inch apart. Then quilt straight lines in the opposite diagonal direction, again spacing the lines 1 inch apart. The lines will cross one another to create a diamond pattern.

31 Carefully trim the edges of the quilt back so that they extend exactly $\frac{5}{8}$ inch beyond the quilt top and batting. Finger-press the raw edges $\frac{1}{4}$ inch to the wrong side, then fold the edges of the quilt back over onto the quilt top and slip-stitch in place using matching thread and mitering the corners neatly.

HIGH-RELIEF APPLIQUÉ

You can emphasize the berries in the middle of the flowers by stuffing them. To do this, cut out twice the number of berries required, adding a $\frac{1}{4}$ inch seam allowance. Stitch 2 berries together with right sides facing and raw edges even. Using sharp scissors, clip into one fabric only (the facing) to make an opening for turning. Turn berry to the right side through the opening; press so that the seam does not show on the right side. Stuff the berry until plump, then lap the cut edges of the opening over one another and whipstitch together. Place the stuffed appliqué in position on the background, facing side down. Slipstitch in place.

F BORDER STRIP

| inches | 4$\frac{1}{2}$ | 13 | 21$\frac{1}{2}$ | 30 | 38$\frac{1}{2}$ | 47 | 55$\frac{1}{2}$ | 64 | 72$\frac{1}{2}$ |

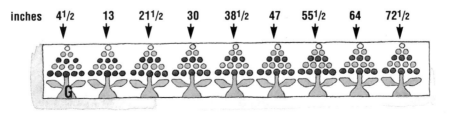

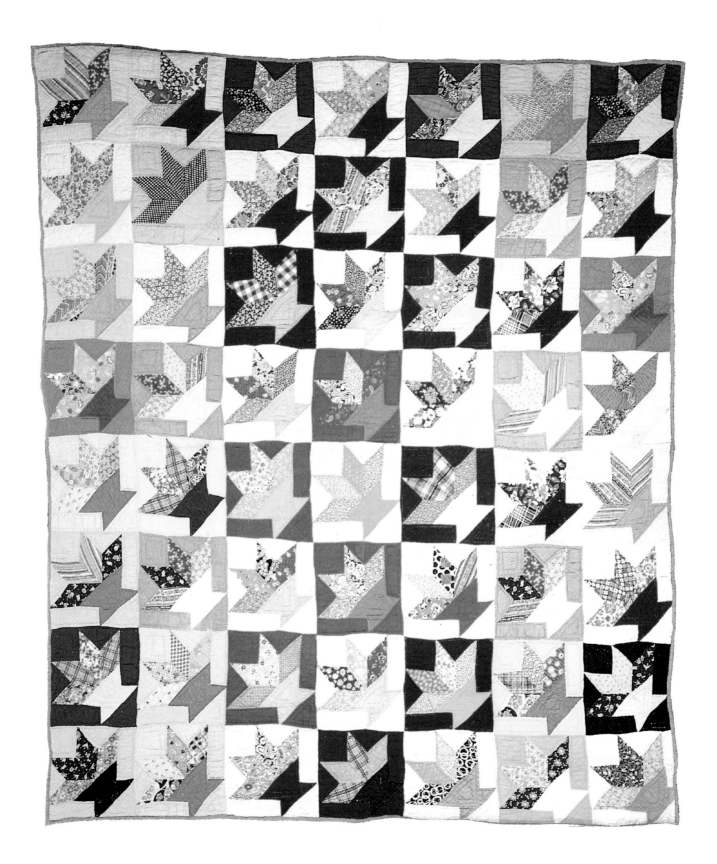

Cactus Basket

Pied Beauty, Gerard Manley Hopkins (1844-1889)

Glory be to God for dappled things –
For skies of couple-colour as a brinded cow;
For rose-moles all in stipple upon trout that swim;
Fresh-firecoal chestnut-falls; finches' wings;
Landscape plotted and pieced – fold, fallow, and plough;
And all trades, their gear and tackle and trim...

The cheerful candy-colored pastels contrast beautifully with the bold primary colors in this quilt. There is a whimsical regularity to the placement of the fabrics that certifies the quilt maker's talent. This is the kind of patchwork quilt that appeals to everyone and works in any setting – a genuine scrap quilt and a true example of American folk art. It was made around 1930 in Iowa.

Cactus Basket

ABILITY LEVEL: INTERMEDIATE

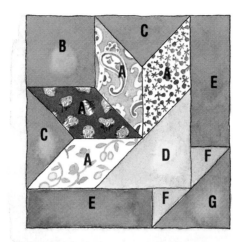

SIZE

Block: 9 1/2 inches square;
56 blocks required
Finished quilt: 66 1/2 x 76 inches

MATERIALS

Note: This is a scrap quilt, where the maker used the fabrics she had on hand to create each block – no two blocks are the same. The yardages that are given below assume that you will be using the same fabric for the background (light), the baskets (dark) and the 'cactus' pieces (medium) throughout the entire quilt; this will result in a very graphic, contemporary effect. If you wish to make a quilt that resembles the antique example shown here, choose an assortment of scrap fabrics, using solids for the background pieces, and contrasting plaids, stripes and prints for the basket and cactus pieces. If you are

making a scrap quilt, refer to the yardages below to give yourself a general idea of how much fabric you'll need to make the quilt.

◆ 3 1/2 yards light fabric
◆ 2 1/2 yards medium fabric
◆ 1 yard dark fabric
◆ 3 3/4 yards fabric for back of quilt
◆ 3/8 yard of coordinating fabric for binding
◆ 67 x 76 1/2 inch piece of batting

CUTTING

Note: A 1/4 inch seam allowance is included in all measurements; templates do not include a seam allowance. Full-size templates can be found on page 115.
Quilt back: 2 pieces, 38 1/2 x 67 inches.
Binding: Cut 7 strips across the full width of the coordinating fabric, each 1 1/2 inches wide; stitch strips together so binding measures 8 yards long.
Blocks: (Number of pieces for a single block are in parenthesis.)

Pattern Piece	Number of Pieces	
A	(2)	112 medium
A (R)	(2)	112 medium
B	(1)	56 light
C	(2)	112 light
D	(1)	56 dark
E	(2)	112 light
F	(2)	112 dark
G	(1)	56 light

PIECING A CACTUS BASKET BLOCK

1 Sew an **A** to a reversed **A**; sew a second pair of **A**'s together in the same manner.

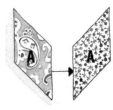

2 Sew the 2 pairs of **A**'s together.

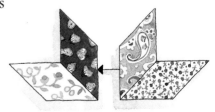

3 Inset a **B** square into the junction between the pairs of **A** pieces; see page 106 for instructions on how to inset.

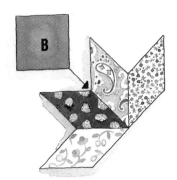

4 Inset a **C** triangle into the remaining 2 angles.

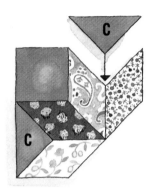

5 Sew a **D** triangle to the straight base of the **A** pieces, forming a square.

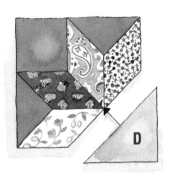

6 Sew an F to one end of each **E**, making 2 pieced strips.

7 Sew an **E-F** strip to each **A-D** edge of the pieced square.

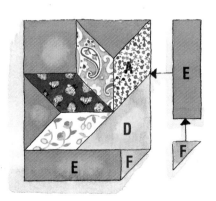

8 Sew a **G** to the **F-F** edge to complete the block.

9 Construct 55 more Cactus Basket blocks in the same manner.

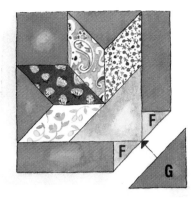

ASSEMBLY

10 Following the **Quilt Plan**, arrange the patchwork blocks in 8 horizontal rows with 7 blocks in each row.

11 Stitch the blocks together in rows, then stitch the rows together, matching seams carefully at the intersections.

12 To construct the quilt back, sew the long edges of the 2 fabric pieces together. Press the seam allowance to one side.

13 Assemble the quilt as directed on page 109.

FINISHING

14 Quilt each Cactus Basket block as shown in the **Quilting Diagram** on page 115.

15 Bind the quilt as directed on pages 110-111.

QUILT PLAN

Autumn

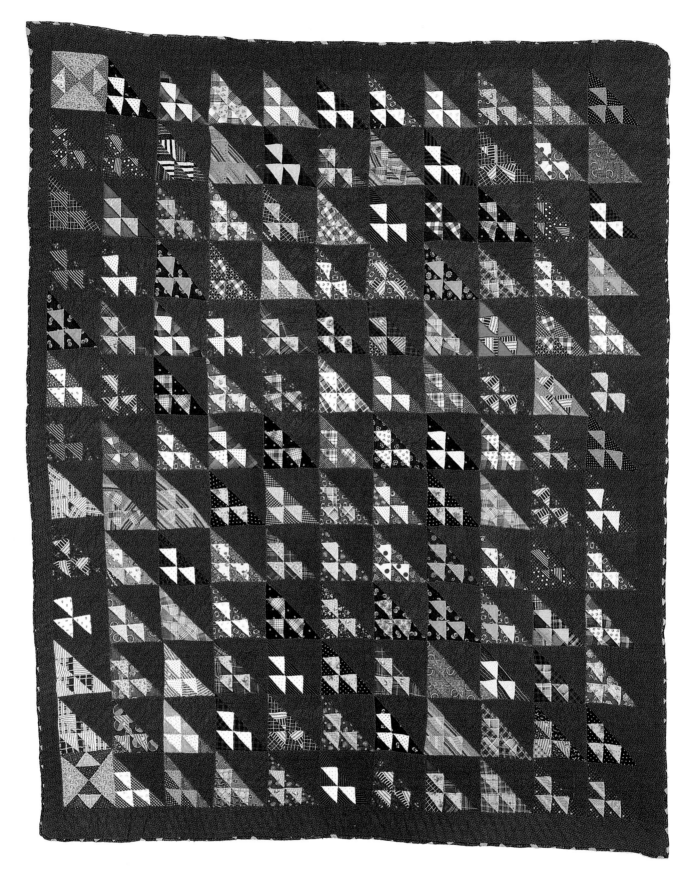

Birds in the Air

Emily Dickinson, (1830 – 1886)

Out of sight? What of that?
See the bird – reach it!
Curve by Curve – Sweep by Sweep –
Round the Steep Air –
Danger! What is that to her?

The light triangles which seem to flutter across the surface of this quilt are evocative of the flight of birds on their autumn migration – hence the name of this traditional patchwork pattern: *Birds in the Air*. It was made around 1890 in North Carolina and displays some of the characteristics of a traditional Appalachian quilt: a dark background fabric and rather large quilting stitches. We'll never know why the quiltmaker chose to include the different patches in two of the corners, but they certainly add to its overall charm.

Birds in the Air

ABILITY LEVEL: BEGINNER

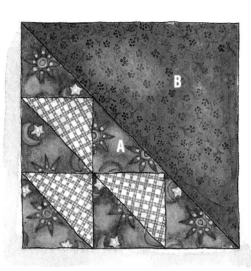

SIZE
Block: 6 inches square;
143 blocks required
Finished quilt: 72 x 84 inches

MATERIALS
◆ 7 yards bright fabric
(includes fabric for borders and
back of quilt)
◆ 2¹/₂ yards dark fabric
◆ 1¹/₄ yards light fabric
◆ ³/₈ yard of coordinating fabric
for binding
◆ 72¹/₂ x 84¹/₂ inch piece of
batting

CUTTING
Note: A ¹/₄ inch seam allowance is
included in all measurements; templates
do not include a seam allowance. Full-size
templates can be found on page 125.

Back of Quilt: 2 pieces, 36¹/₂ x 84¹/₂
inches, bright fabric.

Borders: From bright fabric, cut 2 **C**
strips 3¹/₂ x 78¹/₂ inches and 2 **D** strips
3¹/₂ x 72¹/₂ inches.

Binding: Cut 8 strips across the full width
of the coordinating fabric each 1¹/₂ inches
wide; stitch strips together so binding
measures 9 yards long.

Blocks: (Number of pieces for a
single block are in parenthesis).

Pattern Piece	Number of Pieces
A	(3) 429 light
	(6) 858 dark
B	(1) 143 bright

PIECING

1 Sew one light **A** triangle to a dark **A** along the diagonal
edge to form a square. Repeat twice more for a total of 3 **A-A**
squares.

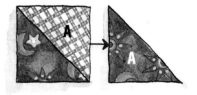

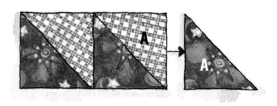

2 Sew a single dark **A** to the light edge of one **A–A** square as
shown in the diagram above right. Set aside.

3 Sew the remaining 2 **A–A** squares together, then sew a
dark A triangle to the light end of the strip as shown.

4 Sew the pieces constructed in steps 2 and 3 together as shown, matching seams carefully. Then sew a dark **A** to the top edge, making a large patchwork triangle.

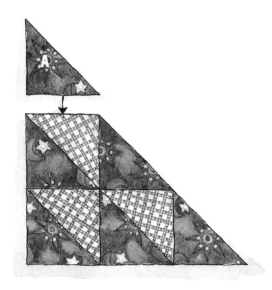

5 Sew the patchwork triangle to a **B** triangle to complete the block.

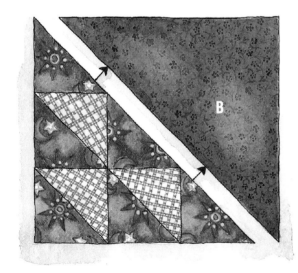

6 Construct 142 more Birds in the Air Blocks in the same manner.

ASSEMBLY

7 Following the **Quilt Plan** and working on a large flat surface, arrange the patchwork blocks in 13 horizontal rows with 11 blocks in each row, placing the patchwork triangle in the same position on each row as shown.

QUILT PLAN

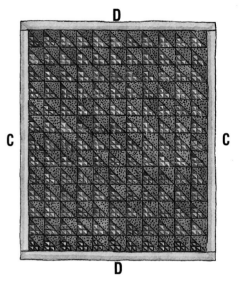

8 Sew the blocks together in rows, pressing the seam allowances in opposite directions on alternate rows.

9 Sew the rows together, matching the seams carefully.

10 Sew the **C** border pieces to the long side edges of the patchwork.

11 Sew the **D** border pieces to the top and bottom edges of the patchwork to complete the quilt top.

12 To construct the quilt back, sew the long edges of the 2 fabric pieces together. Press the seam allowance to one side.

13 Assemble the quilt as directed on page 109.

FINISHING

14 Quilt a small triangle within each **A** triangle, spacing the stitches 1/4 inch away from the sewn seams.

15 Quilt diagonal lines across each **B** triangle, spacing the lines 1/2 inch apart.

16 Bind the quilt as directed on pages 110-111.

Rose Wreath

To Celia, Ben Jonson (?1573-1637)

Drink to me only with thine eyes,
And I will pledge with mine;
Or leave a kiss but in the cup
And I'll not look for wine.
The thirst that from the soul doth rise
Doth ask a drink divine;
But might I of Jove's nectar sup,
I would not change for thine.

I sent thee late a rosy wreath,
Not so much honouring thee
As giving it a hope that there
It could not withered be;
But thou thereon didst only breathe,
And sent'st it back to me;
Since when it grows, and smells, I swear,
Not of itself but thee!

During the 1860's, women used a special dye to create the green shade that was so popular at the time. However, the dye was not stable and as the years passed, the green faded to the soft tan seen in the leaves and vines on this quilt. The color is known as fugitive green. This impressive appliquéd work was made at the end of the last century. One of the edges was cut later, possibly to mend a damaged area, and other repairs have been made over the years. It has been well loved and well used.

Rose Wreath

ABILITY LEVEL: ADVANCED

SIZE
Block: 24 inches square;
9 blocks required
Finished quilt: 72 x 78 inches

MATERIALS
Note: The antique example shown on the previous page would almost certainly have looked like the painted version shown on these pages when it was first made. If you wish to re-create the antique look of the *fugitive green* fabric, choose a tan or khaki colored fabric for the leaves and vines. Alternatively, choose a bright green fabric to duplicate the way the quilt looked before it faded.

◆ $10^1/2$ yards white fabric (includes fabric for back of quilt)
Note: If you use 54 inch wide fabric, you'll need 8 yards.
◆ $4^1/2$ green (tan or khaki) fabric
◆ $2^3/8$ red fabric (includes fabric for binding)

◆ $1/4$ yard gold fabric
◆ $72^1/2$ x $78^1/2$ inch piece of batting

CUTTING
Note: A $1/4$ inch seam allowance is included in all measurements; templates do not include a seam allowance. Full-size templates can be found on page 125.
Quilt back: 2 pieces, $36^1/2$ x $78^1/2$ inches, white fabric.
Background Blocks: From white fabric, cut 9 squares, each $24^1/2$ inches square.
Bias vines: From green or tan fabric, cut one 44 inch and one 15 inch square.

Following the instructions for bias binding on page 108, cut $1^1/2$ inch wide bias strips and sew together to measure 11 yards long. Cut into 9 strips, each 43 inches long for the **A** pieces.
Borders: 2 **H** strips 2 x $72^1/2$ inches, green or tan fabric; 2 **H** strips red fabric.
Binding: Cut 7 strips across the full width of the red fabric, each $1^1/2$ inches wide; stitch strips together so binding measures $8^1/2$ yards long.
Blocks: (Number of pieces for a single block are in parenthesis.)

Pattern Pieces	Number of Pieces	
A	(1)	9 green
B	(4)	36 red
C	(8)	72 green
D	(12)	108 green
D (R)	(12)	108 green
E	(16)	144 red
F	(8)	72 green
G	(4)	36 gold

—— • ◆ • ——

APPLIQUÉING A ROSE WREATH BLOCK
1 Press a background block in half horizontally and vertically, then diagonally. Open up the block and hand-baste along each of the creases. Then press the background block flat again.

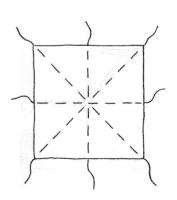

2 Draw a 14 inch diameter circle in the exact middle of the block. If you have a wooden quilting hoop of this size, you can use it instead of a compass.

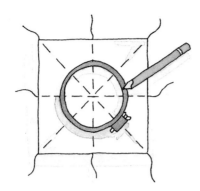

3 Prepare the bias **A** vine for appliqué as directed on page 109. Starting at one of the horizontal basting lines, arrange the vine along the marked line on the background block, easing and pressing it carefully to fit; allow the ends to touch but not overlap; trim away excess fabric. Hand-baste the vine in place along the middle of the strip.

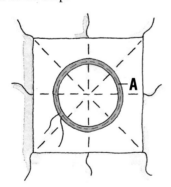

4 Prepare 4 **B** flowers for appliqué as directed on page 107. Position the flowers on the horizontal and vertical basting lines you sewed in Step 1, centering the middle of each flower over

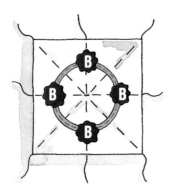

the vine. Appliqué the **B** flowers in place using matching thread. Remove the horizontal and vertical basting lines from the base.

5 Prepare 8 **C** stems for appliqué. Position 4 stems within the vine, exactly on the diagonal basting lines you sewed in Step 1. Baste in place. Set the other 4 stems aside for use in Step 11.

6 Prepare 12 **D** and 12 reversed **D** leaves for appliqué. Position one leaf and its reverse on each side of each of the **C** stems within the vine. Baste in place. Set aside the other leaves for use in steps 8 and 11.

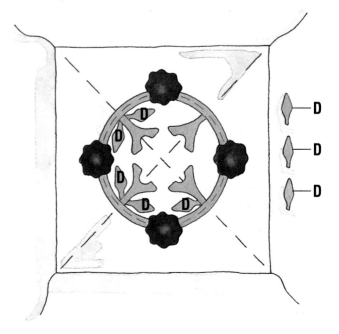

7 Prepare 16 **E** buds for appliqué; you will need 4 buds for this step. Position one bud at the tip of each **C** stem, tucking the base of the bud beneath the stem. Appliqué the **E** buds, **D** leaves and **C** stems in place using matching thread.

8 Prepare 8 **F** stems for appliqué. Position the stems along the outside of the vine, centered between the flowers and the diagonal basting lines on the base as shown. Then position one **D** leaf on the side of 4 stems as shown; position a reversed **D** on the adjacent stems. Baste in place.

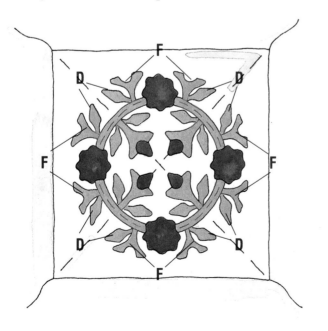

9 Position an **E** bud at the tip of each **F** stem, tucking the base of the bud beneath the stem. Appliqué the **E** buds, **D** leaves and **F** stems in place using matching thread. Prepare 4 **G** circles for appliqué as directed on page 39, then center one **G** circle over each **B** flower. Appliqué the **G** circles and **A** vine in place using matching thread. Remove the basting stitches from the vine.

10 To mark the placement for the corner units, measure 6½ inches from the corner of the base along one of the diagonal basting lines and mark an X as shown in the illustration above; repeat for the other 3 corners.

11 Position a **C** stem in each corner, placing the base of the stem over the marked X as shown at the top of the next page. Position a **D** leaf on each side of each stem. Position one **E** bud at the tip of each **C** stem, tucking the base of the bud beneath the stem. Appliqué the buds, leaves and stems in place using matching thread. Remove the diagonal basting lines.

12 Construct 8 more Rose Wreath blocks in the same manner.

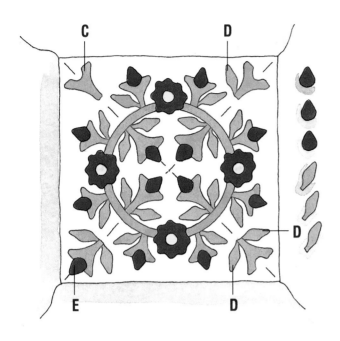

14 Stitch the blocks together in rows.

15 Stitch the rows together, matching seams carefully at the intersections.

16 Stitch a green **H** border to opposite sides of the quilt.

17 Stitch a red **H** border to each green **H** border to complete the quilt top.

18 To construct the quilt back, sew the 2 fabric pieces together along the long edges. Press the seam allowance to one side.

19 Assemble the quilt top, batting and back as directed on page 109.

FINISHING

20 Outline-quilt the appliqué pieces. Quilt along the seams of the border pieces.

21 Bind the quilt with a separate binding as directed on pages 110-111.

ASSEMBLY

13 Following the Quilt Plan and working on a large flat surface, arrange the blocks in 3 horizontal rows with 3 blocks in each row.

QUILT PLAN

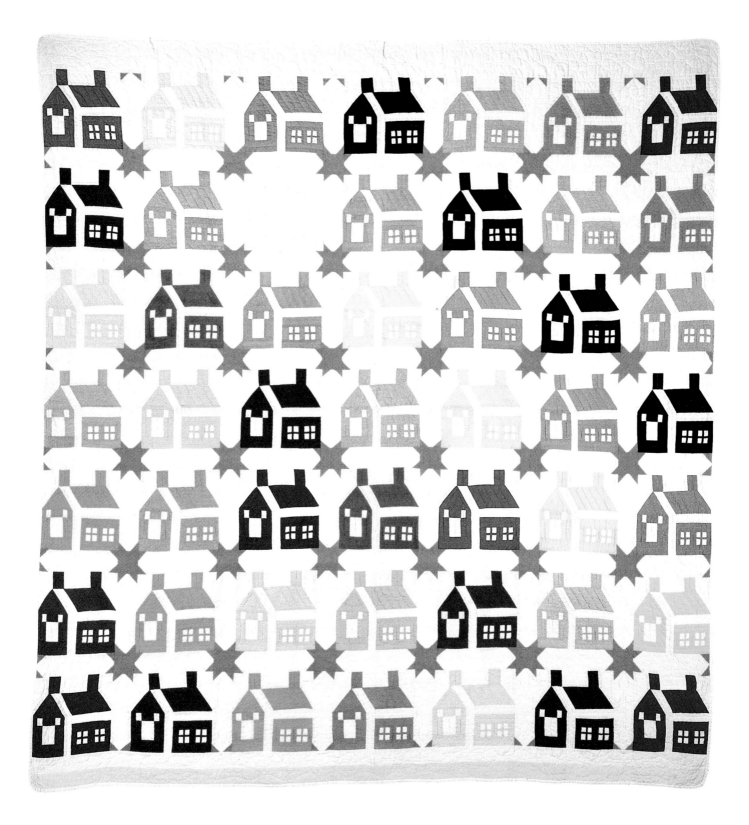

Rainbow Schoolhouses

Among School Children, William Butler Yeats (1865-1939)

I walk through the long schoolroom questioning;
A kind old nun in a white hood replies;
The children learn to cipher and to sing,
To study reading-books and histories,
To cut and sew, be neat in everything...

What a wonderful and imaginative setting the quilt maker has chosen for this fine example of the well loved *Schoolhouse* design. The quilt maker artfully manipulated a rainbow of fabrics and organized them into diagonal bands punctuated by bright pink stars. This is actually a scrap quilt, although it may not look like one, such was the skill of the woman who made it. The quilt dates from 1940.

Rainbow Schoolhouses

ABILITY LEVEL: INTERMEDIATE

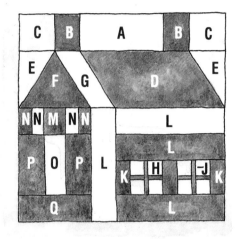

SIZE

Block: 9 inches square;
49 blocks required
Finished quilt: 76^1/$_2$ x 83^1/$_2$ inches

MATERIALS

◆ 9 yards white fabric
(includes fabric for back of quilt and
separate binding)
◆ 1^3/$_8$ yard blue fabric
◆ ^{3}/$_4$ yard yellow fabric
◆ ^{5}/$_8$ yard green fabric
◆ ^{1}/$_2$ yard black fabric
◆ ^{3}/$_4$ yard lavender fabric
◆ 1 yard red fabric
◆ ^{5}/$_8$ yard brown fabric
◆ ^{3}/$_8$ yard orange fabric
◆ ^{3}/$_4$ yard pink fabric
◆ 77 x 84 inch piece of batting

CUTTING

Note: A ^{1}/$_4$ inch seam allowance is
included in all measurements; templates
do not include a seam allowance. Full-size
templates can be found on pages 120-121.
Quilt back: 2 pieces, 38^3/$_4$ x 84 inches,
white fabric.
Borders: One **U** strip 4 x 77 inches, white
fabric; one **V** strip 2^1/$_4$ x 77 inches, white
fabric; one **V** strip, yellow fabric.
Binding: Cut 8 strips across the full
width of the white fabric, each 1^1/$_2$ inches
wide; stitch strips together so binding

measures 9 yards long.
Blocks: (Number of pieces for a single
block are in parenthesis. These cutting
instructions assume that you are making
the antique quilt shown in the photograph
in which there are 12 blue, 6 yellow, 5
green, 4 black, 6 lavender, 8 red, 5 brown
and 3 orange blocks. See also the Quilt
Plan on page 63.)

Pattern Piece	Number of Pieces	
A	(1)	49 white
B	(2)	24 blue, 12 yellow, 10 green, 8 black, 12 lavender, 16 red, 10 brown, 6 orange
C	(2)	98 white
D	(1)	12 blue, 6 yellow, 5 green, 4 black, 6 lavender, 8 red, 5 brown, 3 orange
E	(1)	49 white
E (R)	(1)	49 white
F	(1)	12 blue, 6 yellow, 5 green, 4 black, 6 lavender, 8 red, 5 brown, 3 orange
G	(1)	49 white
H	(2)	98 white
J	(4)	48 blue, 24 yellow, 20 green, 16 black, 24 lavender, 32 red, 20 brown, 12 orange
K	(3)	36 blue, 18 yellow, 15 green, 12 black, 18 lavender, 24 red, 15 brown, 9 orange
L	(2)	98 white, 24 blue, 12 yellow, 10 green, 8 black, 12 lavender, 16 red, 10 brown, 6 orange
M	(1)	12 blue, 6 yellow, 5 green, 4 black, 6 lavender, 8 red, 5 brown, 3 orange
N	(2)	98 white, 24 blue, 12 yellow, 10 green, 8 black, 12 lavender, 16 red, 10 brown, 6 orange
O	(1)	49 white
P	(2)	24 blue, 12 yellow, 10 green, 8 black, 12 lavender, 16 red, 10 brown, 6 orange
Q	(1)	12 blue, 6 yellow, 5 green, 4 black, 6 lavender, 8 red, 5 brown, 3 orange
Sashing		
R		84 white
S		168 pink
S (R)		168 pink
T		36 pink

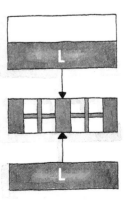

PIECING A SCHOOLHOUSE BLOCK

Note: To avoid confusion when you are piecing the blocks, separate all the pieces for each block into color groups, and then work on one color group at a time. The instructions that follow assume that you will be working with the same color fabric throughout each individual block.

1 To construct the top (chimney) strip of the block, sew a **B** to each side of **A**, then sew a **C** to each **B**.

2 To construct the roof strip, sew an **E** to the right edge of **D**.

3 Sew a reversed **E** to the left edge of **F**.

4 Sew the opposite edges of **F** and **D** to each side of a **G** to complete the roof strip.

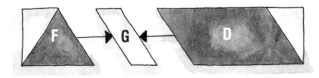

5 Next construct the lower right side of the house. Prepare

the **J** windowpane appliqués by folding each of the long edges of 2 **J**'s ¼ inch to the wrong side; press. Appliqué one **J** horizontally across the exact middle of an **H**.

6 Appliqué the second **J** vertically across the exact middle of **H** on top of the first **J**. Repeat for the second **H** window piece.

7 Sew a **K** to one side edge of each window as shown, sandwiching the raw ends of the appliqués in the seams. Then sew the opposite edges of each window to the remaining **K**.

8 Sew one white **L** to a colored **L**.

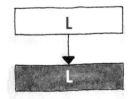

9 Sew the colored edge of the **L-L** strip to the top edge of the window strip, sandwiching the raw ends of the appliqués in the seams. Sew the remaining single colored **L** to the bottom edge of the window strip in the same manner.

10 Sew a white **L** to the left side edge of the window area.

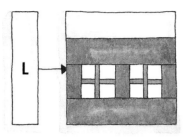

11 Next sew each white **N** to a colored **N**, then sew the white **N**'s to each side of **M**.

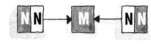

12 Sew a **P** to each long side edge of **O**.

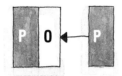

13 Sew the N-M-N strip to the top edge of **P-O-P**; sew a **Q** to the bottom edge.

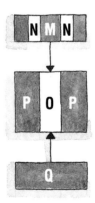

14 Sew the strip just made to the remaining long edge of the white **L** sewn in step 10 to complete the bottom of the house.

15 Sew the chimney strip to the roof strip, then sew the bottom of the house to the roof strip, matching seams carefully, to complete the block.

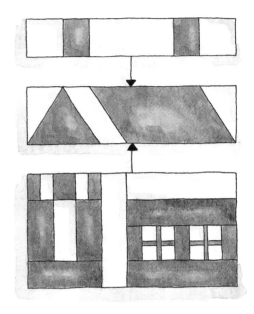

16 Construct 48 more Schoolhouse Blocks in the same manner.

SASHING

17 To construct each sashing rectangle, sew an **S** triangle to each angled edge of an **R** piece. Repeat until you have constructed 84 sashing rectangles.

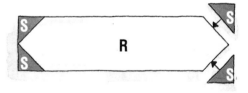

18 Next, construct the horizontal sashing strips. Join 7 sashing rectangles with 6 **T** squares, alternating the pieces as shown in the diagram below to make one long strip. Make 5 more horizontal sashing strips in the same manner.

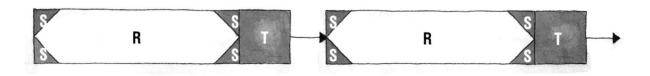

ASSEMBLY

19 Following the **Quilt Plan** and working on a large flat surface, arrange the patchwork blocks with the remaining sashing rectangles and the 6 horizontal sashing strips. You can follow the color scheme as shown on the **Quilt Plan** or make up your own arrangement.

QUILT PLAN

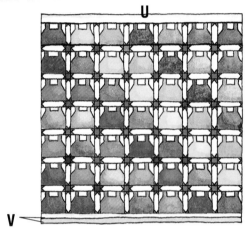

20 Sew the patchwork Schoolhouse blocks to the sashing rectangles to form horizontal rows as shown below.

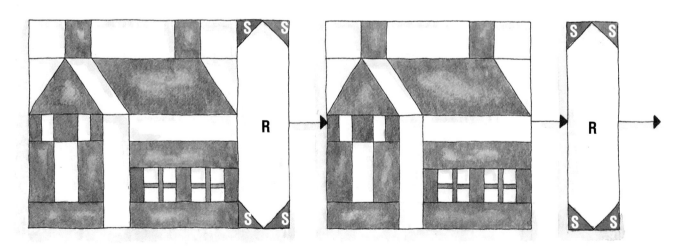

21 Join the patchwork rows to the horizontal sashing rows, matching the seams carefully at the intersections; pink stars will form where the **S** and **T** pieces meet.

22 Sew the white **U** strip to the top edge of the patchwork.

23 Sew the long edge of the yellow **V** border to the white **V** border, then sew the white **V** border to the bottom edge of the patchwork to complete the quilt top.

24 To construct the quilt back, sew the long edges of the 2 fabric pieces together. Press the seam allowance to one side.

25 Assemble the quilt top, batting and back as directed on page 109.

FINISHING

26 Quilt the patchwork schoolhouses as shown in the **Quilting Diagram** on page 121.

27 Trace the full-size flower and leaf quilting pattern from the **R** pattern, and make a template as directed on page 110. Transfer the design to the middle of each of the **R** pieces. Quilt the design.

28 Transfer the flower only to the middle of each **T** square; quilt the flowers.

29 Transfer the flower and leaf design across each of the border pieces; quilt.

30 Bind the quilt with a separate binding as directed on pages 110-111.

Winter

Evergreen

The Visionary, Emily Brontë (1818-1848)

Silent is the house: all are laid asleep:
One alone looks out o'er the snow-wreaths deep,
Watching every cloud, dreading every breeze
That whirls the wildering drift, and bends the groaning trees.

Evergreen trees march in stately procession across the surface of this quilt – and seemingly beyond its borders. The formality of the quilt set is balanced by the jolly tree shapes, creating a marvelous impression of Christmas and snow and cool forests. Made in Texas in the 1920's, the design is one of the many commercial patchwork patterns that appeared regularly in women's magazines and in newspapers during the 1920's and 1930's.

Evergreen

ABILITY LEVEL: INTERMEDIATE

SIZE

Block: 9 inches square; 54 complete blocks, 21 half blocks and 2 corner blocks required

Finished quilt: 63¾ x 83 inches

MATERIALS

◆ 8¼ yards white fabric (includes fabric for back of quilt)

◆ 5¼ yards green fabric (includes fabric for binding)

◆ ¼ yard brown fabric

◆ 64¼ x 83½ inch piece of batting

CUTTING

Note: A ¼ inch seam allowance is included in all measurements; templates do not include a seam allowance. Full-size templates can be found on page 124.

Quilt back: 2 pieces, 42 x 64¼ inches, white fabric

Binding: Cut 7 strips across full width of green fabric, each 2 inches wide; stitch strips together so binding measures yards long.

Blocks: (Number of pieces for a single block are in parenthesis.)

Pattern Piece	Number of Pieces	
A	(1)	58 green
B	(1)	58 white
B (R)	(1)	58 white
C	(2)	116 green
D	(1)	58 white
D (R)	(1)	58 white
E	(1)	58 green
F	(1)	58 white
F (R)	(1)	58 white
G	(1)	59 green
H	(1)	59 white
H (R)	(1)	59 white
J	(1)	59 white
J (R)	(1)	59 white
K	(1)	59 brown
L	(1)	59 white
L (R)	(1)	59 white
M	(2)	132 white

Border-Blocks (Sides and Corners):

B	7 white
B (R)	7 white
D	7 white
D (R)	7 white
F	7 white
F (R)	7 white
H	6 white
H (R)	6 white
J	6 white
J (R)	6 white
L	6 white
L (R)	6 white
N	7 green
N (R)	7 green
O	13 green
O (R)	13 green
P	7 green
P (R)	7 green
Q	6 green
Q (R)	6 green
R	12 brown
S	13 white
S (R)	13 white

— • ◆ • —

PIECING AN EVERGREEN BLOCK

1 Sew a **B** and a reversed **B** to opposite sides of **A**.

2 Sew a **D** and a reversed **D** to opposite sides of **C**.

3 Sew an **F** and a reversed **F** to opposite sides of **E**.

4 Sew an **H** and a reversed **H** to opposite sides of **G**.

5 Sew a **J** and a reversed **J** to opposite sides of **C**.

6 Sew an **L** and a reversed **L** to opposite sides of **K**.

7 Join the pieces that comprise the top half of the block as shown. Sew an **M** triangle to the **B-A-B** strip.

8 Join the pieces that comprise the bottom half of the block as shown. Sew an **M** triangle to the **L-K-L** strip.

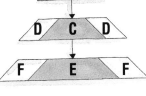

9 Sew the top and bottom halves of the patchwork together.

10 Construct 53 more complete Evergreen blocks.

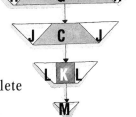

PIECING THE BORDER BLOCKS

11 For the top and bottom borders of the quilt, assemble 4 blocks as directed above, but omit Step 9 – simply leave the half blocks separate. Then construct one additional bottom half of a block using the remaining patchwork pieces. (**Note:** Only 4 top halves of the block are required.)

12 To construct the half-blocks for the sides of the quilt, sew **B** to **N**, **D** to **O**, **F** to **P**, **H** to **Q**, **J** to **O** and **L** to **R**. Sew these strips together, then sew an **S** to the top and bottom edges. Construct 5 more blocks in the same way, then 6 blocks in reverse.

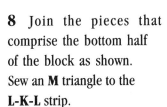

13 To construct the blocks for the bottom corners of the quilt, sew **B** to **N**, **D** to **O** and **F** to **P**. Sew these strips together, then sew an **S** to the top edge. Construct a second corner block in reverse.

ASSEMBLY

14 Following the Quilt Plan, arrange the patchwork blocks on point to create 12 horizontal rows, alternating 4 blocks in one row with 5 blocks in the adjacent row.

15 Position the half-blocks for the tree bottoms along the top edge of the quilt; position the half-blocks for the tree tops along the bottom edge.

16 Fill in the side edges with the vertical half-blocks.

17 Put the corner blocks in the bottom left and right corners.

18 Sew the patchwork blocks together in diagonal rows; sew a half- or quarter-block to each end of each row.

19 Join the diagonal rows together, starting with the long middle rows, and working outward to the corners.

20 To construct the quilt back, sew the long edges of the 2 fabric pieces together. Press the seam allowance to one side.

21 Assemble the quilt as directed on page 109.

FINISHING

22 Starting in the middle and working outward, work quilting stitches 'in the ditch' in horizontal rows. Outline-quilt each of the evergreen trees.

23 Bind quilt with a separate binding as directed on pages 110-111.

Double Irish Chain

To Ireland in the Coming Times, William Butler Yeats (1865-1939)

*Know, that I would accounted be
True brother of that company,
Who sang to sweeten Ireland's wrong,
Ballad and story, rann and song;
Nor be I any less of them,
Because the red-rose-bordered hem
Of her, whose history began
Before God made the angelic clan,*

*Trails all about the written page;
For in the world's first blossoming age
The light fall of her flying feet
Made Ireland's heart begin to beat;
And still the starry candles flare
To help her light foot here and there;
And still the thoughts of Ireland brood
Upon her holy quietude.*

Made in the turkey red, green and white colors that were so popular during the 1860's, this magnificent *Double Irish Chain* quilt has fine cross-hatched quilting over its entire surface. The unusual diamond border adds a raffish quality to this otherwise conventional design. It was made in Delaware County, Pennsylvania.

Double Irish Chain

ABILITY LEVEL: BEGINNER

SIZE
Block: 10 inches square; 32 No. 1 blocks and 32 No. 2 blocks required
Finished quilt: 88 inches square

MATERIALS
◆ 11 yards white fabric (includes fabric for back of quilt and separate binding)
◆ 3 yards red fabric
◆ 1¾ yards green fabric (see **Note** under **Borders** below right)
◆ 88½ inch square piece of batting
◆ Template for **E**: 6½ x 10½ inches

CUTTING
Note: The central portion of this quilt can be made quickly and easily without the use of templates. You can use a rotary cutter and ruler to cut the strips, or you can mark the fabrics with a pencil and ruler and cut the strips using scissors. See the instructions on page 105 for using a rotary cutter. The measurements that follow assume that your fabric is

45 inches wide; cut off ½ inch at each selvage edge for a total width of 44 inches (**Exception:** see **Note** under **Borders** below – 4 green strips must be cut 44½ inches wide). All measurements include a ¼ inch seam allowance; templates do not include a seam allowance. Full-size templates for the border pieces can be found on page 125.
Quilt back: One central panel, 44 x 88½ inches, white fabric and 2 side panels, 22¾ x 88½ inches, white fabric.
Borders (**Note:** The fabric requirements given above allow for pieced borders; if you do not wish to piece the borders, you must buy 3¾ yards of green fabric.): for **H**, cut 4 strips 2 x 43 inches (or 2 **H** strips 2 x 85½ inches), green fabric; for **J**, cut 4 strips 2 x 44½ inches (or 2 **J** strips 2 x 88½ inches), green fabric.
Binding: Cut 9 strips across the full width of the white fabric, each 1½ inches wide;

stitch strips together so binding measures 10 yards long.
Fabric Strips Required:
Measure and cut strips across the entire width of the fabrics, each 2½ inches wide.
White: 12
Red: 32
Green: 18
Pieced Strips Required:
(Number of strips for a single block are in parenthesis.)

Pattern Piece	Number of Pieces	
Block No. 1:		
A	(2)	64
B	(2)	64
C	(1)	32
Block No. 2:		
D	(2)	64
E	(1)	32
Border:		
F		128 red
G		264 white
		8 red

PIECING A NO.1 BLOCK

1 To construct the **A** strips, you'll need 4 white strips, 8 red strips and 8 green strips. Stitch the strips together as shown to create 4 pieced fabrics, each 10½ inches deep. Measure and cut 17 strips, each 2½ inches wide, from each width of pieced fabric, until you have a total of 64 **A** strips (you only need to cut 13 strips from the last width of pieced fabric).

3 To construct the **C** strips, you'll need 4 white strips, 4 red strips and 2 green strips. Stitch the strips together, alternating colors as shown to create 2 pieced fabrics, each 10½ inches deep. Measure and cut 16 strips, each 2½ inches wide, from each width of pieced fabric, until you have a total of 32 **C** strips.

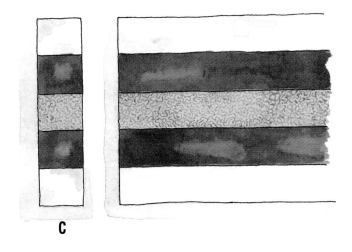

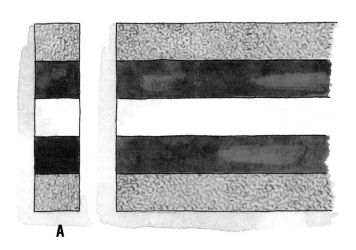

A

4 Stitch a **B** strip to each side of a **C** strip, matching seams carefully.

2 To construct the **B** strips, you'll need 12 red strips and 8 green strips. Stitch the strips together, alternating the colors as shown to create 4 pieced fabrics, each 10½ inches deep. Measure and cut 17 strips, each 2½ inches wide, from each width of pieced fabric, until you have a total of 64 **B** strips (you only need to cut 13 strips from the last width of pieced fabric).

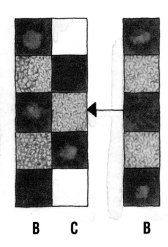

B   **C**   **B**

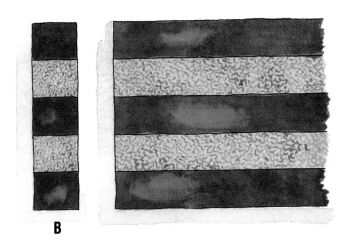

B

5 Stitch an **A** strip to each **B** strip, matching seams carefully, to complete Block No. 1 as shown in the illustration overleaf.

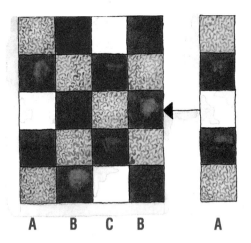

A   B   C   B   A

6 Construct 31 more Double Irish Chain No. 1 blocks in the same manner.

PIECING A NO.2 BLOCK

7 To construct the **D** strips, you'll need 8 red strips. Cut 4 strips, each 6½ inch wide, across the entire width of the white fabric. Stitch the strips together as shown to create 4 pieced fabrics, each 10½ inches deep. Measure and cut 17 strips, each 2½ inches wide as shown in the illustration above right, from each width of pieced fabric, until you have a total of 64 **D** strips (you only need to cut 13 strips from the last width of pieced fabric).

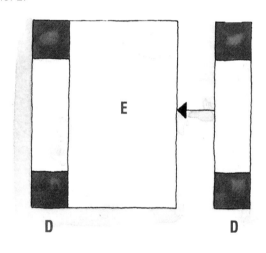

D   E

8 Stitch a **D** strip to each long edge of an **E** piece to complete Block No. 2.

D   E   D

9 Construct 31 more Double Irish Chain No. 2 blocks in the same manner.

PIECED INNER BORDERS

10 For the top border, stitch a **G** triangle to opposite sides of 31 **F** squares as shown; stitch these diagonally-shaped strips to each other, matching the seam allowances carefully where the points of the **F** squares meet. Stitch a red and a white **G** triangle to each end of the strip to square the ends. This will create a top border strip that is 80½ inches long. Construct the bottom border strip in the same manner.

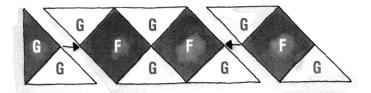

11 For the side borders, stitch 68 **G** triangles to 33 **F** squares as you did in Step 10; stitch a red and a white **G** triangle to each end of the strip to square the ends. This will create a side border strip that is 85½ inches long. Make the second side border strip in the same manner.

ASSEMBLY

12 Following the **Quilt Plan**, arrange the patchwork No. 1 blocks with the No. 2 blocks to form a checkerboard pattern, making 8 rows with 8 blocks in each row.

13 Stitch the blocks together in horizontal rows.

14 Stitch the rows together, matching seams carefully at the intersections.

15 Stitch the top and bottom pieced border strips to the patchwork.

16 Stitch the side border strips to the patchwork.

17 If you are piecing the borders, stitch 2 pairs of **H** pieces together to construct the 2 **H** borders. Stitch the **H** borders to the top and bottom edges of the patchwork.

18 If you are piecing the borders, stitch 2 pairs of **J** pieces together to construct the 2 **J** borders. Stitch the **J** borders to the side edges of the patchwork to complete the quilt top.

19 To construct the quilt back, sew the long edges of the side panels to each side of the central panel. Press the seam allowances to one side.

20 Assemble the quilt as directed on page 109.

FINISHING

21 Using a pencil or chalk, draw a straight diagonal line connecting the opposite corners of the quilt. Repeat this line in the other direction so that you have drawn an X across the quilt.

22 Quilt along these marked lines, then work parallel lines of quilting to the left and right of these lines, spacing the lines 2 inches apart. Where the quilting lines cross, they will create a cross-hatch pattern.

23 Bind the quilt as directed on pages 110-111.

QUILT PLAN

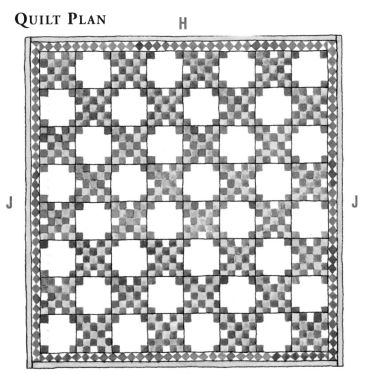

Oak Leaf and Reel

The Old Oak Tree, W. H. Davies (1871-1940)

I sit beneath your leaves, old oak,
You mighty one of all the trees;
Within whose hollow trunk a man
Could stable his big horse with ease.

A presentation quilt was a popular way to commemorate important events during the mid-19th century, and was often made by a group of women as a gift for a local dignitary. This magnificent work of art was a presentation quilt, made in Pennsylvania circa 1850. An inscription around the middle appliqué reads "A Donation to the Rev John Farquhar from the Ladies of the Chanceford Congregation." The appliqué work is exquisite and the quilting perfect – the only touch of eccentricity being the slightly asymmetrical bows and tassels around the border.

Oak Leaf and Reel
ABILITY LEVEL: ADVANCED

SIZE
Block: 16½ inches square;
25 blocks required
Finished quilt: 98½ inches square

MATERIALS
◆ 13¼ yards white fabric (includes fabric for back of quilt and fold-finished edge)
◆ 3¾ yards blue fabric
◆ 4 yards red fabric
◆ 99 x 99 inch piece of batting

CUTTING
Note: A ¼ inch seam allowance is included in all measurements; templates do not include a seam allowance. Full-size templates can be found on pages 116-117.

Quilt back: From white fabric cut one central panel, 44 x 99 inches, and 2 side panels, 28 x 99 inches.
Background squares: 25 squares, each 17 x 17 inches square, white fabric.

Borders: 2 **J** strips 8½ x 83 inches, white fabric; 2 **K** strips 8½ x 99 inches, white fabric.
Blocks: (Number of pieces for a single block are in parenthesis.)

Pattern Piece	Number of Pieces	
A	(4)	52 red
	(4)	48 blue
B	(1)	12 red
	(1)	13 blue
Border:		
C		32 red
D		32 blue
E		28 blue
F		28 blue
G		4 blue
H		4 blue

•◆•

PIECING AN OAK LEAF AND REEL BLOCK
Note: As you appliqué the blocks, make sure that you always combine the red crescents with the blue leaves and the blue crescents with the red leaves.

1 First prepare a base for the appliqués. Fold a background square in half diagonally first in one direction and then the other; press carefully. Open out the block and hand-baste a row of stitches along each of the diagonal folds. Press the base to remove the folds.

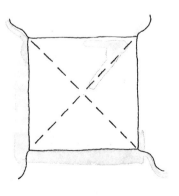

2 Prepare 4 **A** crescents for appliqué as directed on page 107. Position a crescent on the base in each of the 4 quadrants delineated by your basting stitches; pin in place.

3 Prepare one **B** leaf section for appliqué as directed on pages 107-108. Alternatively, because the leaves in each of the 4 quadrants of this appliqué are not easy to manipulate, you may wish to prepare the appliqué in a different way as follows: Clip into the seam allowances along the curved areas, and then baste or pin the appliqué to the background without pressing

the edges under. You can then turn the raw edges under as you are actually sewing the appliqué in place on the background square, using the tip of your sewing needle to do the actual turning, and holding the folded edges in position with your thumb while you sew them. It will probably be easier to achieve smooth curves on the complex **B** appliqués by using this method.

4 Position the **B** appliqué on the base so that the stems fit neatly between the points of the crescents; adjust the position of the crescents slightly if necessary. Baste in place.

5 Appliqué the **A** and **B** pieces to the base using matching thread. Remove the basting.

6 Construct 24 more Oak Leaf and Reel blocks in the same manner, making a total of 13 blocks with blue leaves and red crescents, and 12 blocks with red leaves and blue crescents.

ASSEMBLY

7 Following the **Quilt Plan** and working on a large flat surface, arrange the patchwork blocks in 5 horizontal rows with 5 blocks in each row. Alternate the blocks to make a checkerboard pattern with the colours as shown (the blocks with the blue leaves will form an X across the quilt).

QUILT PLAN

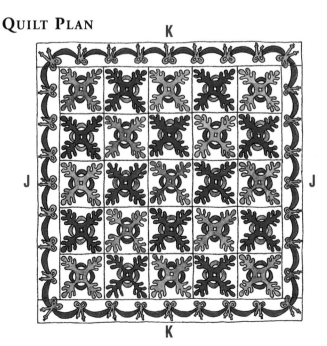

8 Stitch the blocks together in rows.

9 Stitch the rows together, matching seams carefully at the intersections.

BORDERS

10 Stitch a **J** border to each side of the pieced and appliquéd quilt top.

11 Stitch a **K** border to the top and bottom edges of the quilt top.

12 Arrange the **C** crescents on the border pieces, fitting 8 along each side of the quilt. Adjust the space between the crescents as necessary to fit them evenly along the borders. Pin in place.

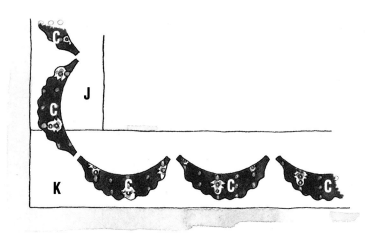

13 Prepare pieces **D**, **E** and **F** for appliqué. These pieces will comprise the tasselled bows along each of the 4 sides of the quilt. Position a **D** piece over the space between the crescents as shown above right.

14 Position **E** and **F** beneath **D** as shown, tucking the ends of the tassels beneath **D**. Appliqué in place using matching thread. Repeat for the remaining bow and tassel appliqués around the borders of the quilt. You will have 4 **D** bows left over for the corners of the quilt.

15 Prepare pieces **G** and **H** for appliqué. These pieces (along with the remaining **D** appliqués) will comprise the tasselled bows in each of the 4 corners of the quilt.

16 Position **D** over the space between the crescents in one corner of the quilt top as shown. Position **G** and **H** beneath **D**, tucking the ends of the tassels beneath **D**. Appliqué in place using matching thread. Repeat for the other 3 corners of the quilt.

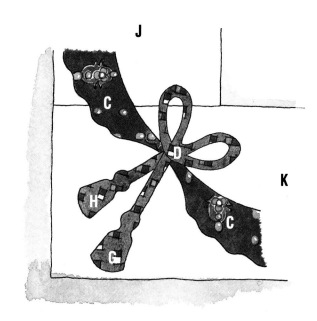

17 Appliqué the **C** crescents to the borders using matching thread.

18 To construct the quilt back, sew the side panels to each long edge of the central panel. Press the seam allowances to one side.

19 Assemble the quilt top, batting and back as directed on page 109.

FINISHING
20 Outline-quilt the leaf and crescent appliqués.

21 Make templates for the fruit and star quilting designs given on page 116. Transfer the fruit design to the quilt top along each of the horizontal seams, centering the design in the slightly oval spaces between the leaves.

22 Transfer the star design to the quilt top along each of the vertical seams, centering the design in the slightly oval spaces between the leaves.

23 Quilt the fruit and star designs.

24 Before you quilt the borders, you must fold-finish the edges of the quilt. First trim the quilt top, batting and back evenly all around. Then fold the edges of the quilt top and the back $1/4$ inch inside and slip-stitch together invisibly using matching thread. Alternatively, if you wish to finish the edges of the quilt with a separate binding, continue quilting the borders, then go on to Step 27.

25 Outline-quilt the bows and crescents around the borders. If you are using a quilting hoop, baste long strips of 6 inch wide fabric to the outer edges of the quilt to make it easier for you to secure the quilt in a hoop.

26 If desired, quilt diagonal parallel lines all around the border, spacing the lines $1/2$ inch apart.

27 If you wish to add a separate binding, you will need $3/8$ yard of the red or blue fabric. Cut 9 strips across the full width of the fabric, each $1^1/2$ inches wide; stitch the strips together so that the total length of the binding measures 11 yards long. Prepare the binding and stitch it to the edges of the quilt as directed on pages 110-111.

Projects

If making a large quilt seems a bit daunting, you can try one of the small projects featured in this section; each one is quick and easy to construct. The photographs of the finished projects illustrate how different each of the designs can look when created in an alternate color scheme.

Frilly Cushion

ABILITY LEVEL:
INTERMEDIATE

Spring Bouquet

SIZE

Block: 12^1/$_2$ inches square;
1 block required
Finished cushion: about 18 inches
square, excluding ruffle

MATERIALS

◆ ^{3}/$_4$ yard pale pink fabric (includes fabric for back of cushion)
◆ ^{5}/$_8$ yard medium pink fabric (includes fabric for ruffle)
◆ ^{3}/$_8$ yard green fabric (includes fabric for piping)
◆ scrap dark pink fabric
◆ scrap white fabric
◆ scrap purple print fabric
◆ scrap lavender fabric
◆ small scrap pink / white print fabric
◆ scrap yellow fabric
◆ 18^1/$_2$ inch square piece of batting
◆ 18^1/$_2$ inch square of plain fabric for quilting the cushion front (this fabric will be hidden inside)
◆ 74 inch length of cotton piping cord
◆ 12 inch pale pink zipper
◆ 18 inch square pillow form

CUTTING

Note: A ^{1}/$_4$ inch seam allowance is included in all measurements; templates do not include a seam allowance. Full-size templates for the Spring Bouquet design can be found on pages 112-113.

Cushion back: From pale pink fabric, cut one piece, 18^1/$_2$ x 16^1/$_2$ inches, and one piece 18^1/$_2$ x 3 inches.

Background square: 13 x 13 inches, pale pink fabric.

Corner Triangles: Cut 2 squares from the pale pink fabric, each 10 x 10 inches. Cut each square in half diagonally to make 4 corner triangles.

Ruffle: Cut 3 strips across the full width of the medium pink fabric, each 6 inches wide.

Piping: Cut 2 strips across the full width of the green fabric, each 1 inch wide; stitch strips together so piping strip measures 74 inches long.

Bias binding for stems: Cut 6 stems on the bias of the green fabric following the chart below. You will need a total length of 18^1/$_2$ inches of bias.

Stem	Length
1	3^1/$_4$ inches
2	5^3/$_4$ inches
3	5^1/$_4$ inches
4	1^1/$_2$ inches
5	1 inch
6	1^3/$_4$ inches

Block:

Pattern Piece	Number of Pieces
A	1 purple print
B	5 dark pink
C	1 green
D	1 green
	6 white
E	4 green
F	1 lavender
G	1 medium pink
H	1 white
J	1 lavender
K	1 pink / white print
L	1 yellow
	1 medium pink
M	2 yellow
N	1 medium pink

APPLIQUÉ

1 Appliqué one Spring Bouquet block as directed on pages 16-19.

2 Arrange the block on a flat surface with the corner triangles as shown in the **Assembly Diagram**.

3 Sew a corner triangle to opposite sides of the block. Sew the remaining 2 corner triangles to the block.

ASSEMBLY

4 Assemble the cushion front, the batting and the fabric for quilting as directed on page 109.

5 Outline-quilt each of the appliqué pieces. Quilt in the ditch along the seams connecting the corner triangles to the appliquéd block.

ASSEMBLY DIAGRAM

corner triangle

6 Trace a full-size pattern for the **B** flower and its center; when tracing, connect the petals to the flower center to make one design unit. Make into a template as directed on page 110. Use the template to transfer the outlines of the design to the center of each of the corner triangles.

7 Quilt along each of the marked flower outlines.

8 Sew the piping to the cushion front following the instructions on page 111.

9 For the ruffle, sew the short ends of the 6 inch strips together to create one continuous circle of fabric; press the seam allowances open. Fold the strip in half lengthwise with wrong sides facing and raw edges even; press.

10 Fold the fabric strip into quarters and mark each of the 4 folds using pins. Sew 2 rows of machine basting $1/4$ inch and $1/8$ inch away from the raw edges all

around, breaking your stitching before and after each of the pins. Gently pull the basting stitches to gather the ruffle evenly into 4 sections, each measuring approximately 18 inches.

11 Arrange the ruffle on the right side of the cushion front, matching the pins to each corner. Pin the ruffle to the cushion, adjusting the gathers evenly and allowing a generous fold at each corner.

CUSHION BACK

12 With right sides facing, raw edges even and making a $1/2$ inch seam, sew the long edges of the 2 rectangles together, using regular stitching for $3^1/4$ inches, changing to basting for 12 inches and changing back to regular stitches for the last $3^1/4$ inches. Press the seam allowance open.

13 Following the instructions on page 111, insert the zipper into the basted portion of the seam.

FINISHING

14 With right sides facing and raw edges even all around, pin the cushion back to the front, sandwiching the ruffle and piping in between. (Leave the zipper partially open to facilitate turning the cushion cover to the right side.)

15 Using a zipper foot, stitch the pieces together all around, sewing as close to the piping cord as possible.

16 Turn to the right side and insert a pillow form, adjusting the corners to fit into each corner of the cushion cover.

Placemat

Art Deco Fans

ABILITY LEVEL:
INTERMEDIATE

SIZE

Block: 7¹/₂ inches square;
1 block required
Finished placemat: 10 x 16 inches

MATERIALS (FOR ONE PLACEMAT AND NAPKIN)

- ³/₈ yard light yellow fabric (includes fabric for back of placemat and napkin)
- ¹/₄ yard navy plaid fabric
- scraps of 3 navy print fabrics
- scraps of 3 yellow print fabrics
- ¹/₈ yard solid navy fabric for binding
- 10¹/₂ x 16¹/₂ inch piece of batting

CUTTING

Note: A ¹/₄ inch seam allowance is included in all measurements; templates do not include a seam allowance. Full-size templates can be found on page 123.
F: 3 x 8 inches, navy plaid fabric.
G: 9 x 10¹/₂ inches, navy plaid fabric.
Back: 10¹/₂ x 16¹/₂ inches, light yellow fabric.
Binding: Cut 2 strips across the full width of the navy fabric, each 1¹/₂ inches wide; stitch strips together so binding measures 1¹/₂ yards.
Napkin: 10¹/₂ x 10¹/₂ inches square, light yellow fabric.

Art Deco Fan Block:

Pattern Piece	Number of Pieces
A	1 navy print
A(R)	1 yellow print
B	1 yellow print
B(R)	1 navy print
C	1 navy print
C(R)	1 yellow print
D	1 light yellow
E	1 navy plaid

ASSEMBLY DIAGRAM

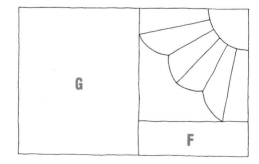

PIECING

1 Piece an Art Deco Fan block as directed on pages 22-23.

2 Sew **F** to the top of the block as shown in the **Assembly Diagram**.

3 Sew **G** to the side of the block to complete the front of the placemat.

ASSEMBLY

4 Assemble the front of the placemat, the batting and the fabric for the back as directed on page 109.

5 Follow the quilting lines on the templates to quilt the block.

6 Follow the lines of the plaid fabric to quilt the **F** and **G** pieces. You can work as much quilting as you wish, provided that you do not leave an area larger than 2 inches unquilted.

7 Bind the quilt with a separate binding as directed on pages 110-111.

NAPKIN

8 Fold the raw edges of the light yellow fabric square ¹/₈ inch to the wrong side and press. Fold again, enclosing the raw edges and press. Topstitch the raw edges in place.

Pot Holder

ABILITY LEVEL: BEGINNER

Cactus Basket

SIZE:
Pot Holder: 10 inches square;
1 block required

MATERIALS

Note: This project is suitable for using up your fabric scraps. The largest scrap you'll need will be a 10 inch square for the back of the pot holder; try to find a heat-resistant fabric in your local fabric shop. You can make the Cactus Basket block shown here, or choose any of the other block designs in this book; if you choose another design, be sure to adjust the measurements of the back, padding and binding pieces. Full-size templates for Cactus Basket can be found on page 115.

◆ scraps of several coordinating 100% cotton fabrics

◆ scrap coordinating fabric for binding: cut enough strips of the coordinating fabric, each 1½ inches wide, and stitch together so binding measures 1¼ yards long.

◆ 10 inch square heat-resistant fabric for back of pot holder

◆ 2 pieces of 100% cotton or wool batting, each 10 inches square

PIECING OR APPLIQUÉ

1 Piece or appliqué one block as directed in the individual instructions for that design; press the block carefully.

2 Place the square of fabric for the back on a flat surface, wrong side up.

3 Place the two pieces of cotton or wool batting on the fabric square, then place the block, right side up, on top of the padding pieces.

4 Pin or baste the layers together firmly, then quilt the block by hand or machine.

5 Following the directions for a separate binding on page 110, apply the binding to the pot holder starting in one corner rather than in the middle of one side edge.

6 After all the edges of the pot holder have been bound, excess binding will extend beyond the starting corner. Machine-stitch the long pressed edges of this extension together, then fold the end under twice to hide the raw edges.

7 Stitch the folded end of the binding to the back of the pot holder to form a loop for hanging.

ASSEMBLY DIAGRAM

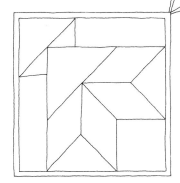

Baby Quilt

ABILITY LEVEL: ADVANCED BEGINNER

SIZE
Finished quilt: 43 inches square

MATERIALS
◆ 2¹/₂ yards white-on-white print fabric (includes fabric for back of quilt)
◆ ³/₄ yard green fabric (includes fabric for binding)
◆ ¹/₄ yard red/orange fabric
◆ ¹/₄ yard medium orange fabric
◆ ¹/₄ yard light orange fabric
◆ scrap gold print fabric
◆ scrap pale yellow fabric
◆ 43¹/₂ x 43¹/₂ inch piece of batting

CUTTING
Note: A ¹/₄ inch seam allowance is included in all measurements; templates do not include a seam allowance. Full-size templates can be found on page 122.
Quilt front and back: 2 pieces, 43¹/₂ x 43¹/₂ inches, white fabric.
Binding: Cut 4 strips across the full width of the green fabric, each 1¹/₂ inches wide; stitch strips together so binding measures 5 yards long.

Love Apple Appliqués:

Pattern Pieces	Number of Pieces
A	5 light orange
B	6 green
C	8 gold print
	16 light orange
D	8 medium orange
	16 red/orange
E	12 green
E(R)	12 green
F	24 green
G	5 pale yellow

APPLIQUÉ
Note: This baby quilt uses the design elements of·the Love Apple quilt, but in a different arrangement, as shown in the **Assembly Diagram** opposite.

1 Read the instructions on pages 26-29 for how to appliqué a Love Apple block. Prepare all the pieces for appliqué as directed.

2 Next, prepare a base for the appliqués. Fold one square of fabric (for the quilt front) in half horizontally and vertically; press carefully. Open out the fabric and hand-baste a row of stitches along each of the folds. Press the base to remove the folds. Next, press the base diagonally in each direction and hand-baste along the folds. Then press the base to remove the folds.

3 Measure 11¾ inches away from the center point (where the basting lines cross in the middle) along the horizontal and vertical basted lines and mark an X for the placement of the **A** appliqués. Position an **A** flower over each of the marked X's and baste in place.

4 Position the remaining **A** flower in the middle of the background, centered exactly over the place where the basting lines cross. Baste, then appliqué each of the flowers in place using matching thread.

5 Position 2 **B** appliqués on the background above and below the middle **A** flower, with the middle of each B centered between the top and bottom flowers. Baste the **B** pieces in place along the middle of each appliqué.

6 Next position the **B** appliqués in the corners. Measure 17 inches along a diagonal basting line from one corner and mark an X. Position the exact middle of a **B** stem over the marked X, with the tips of the stem curving toward the corner as shown in the **Assembly Diagram.** Baste the **B** stem in place along the middle of the appliqué. Repeat for the other 3 corners.

7 Arrange the gold print **C** pieces on each side of the tips of the 2 **central B** stems, tucking the inner curved edges of **C** beneath **B**. Pin in place. Arrange the light orange **C** pieces around the **corner B** stems in the same manner.

8 Arrange the medium orange **D** appliqués on each side of the **central C** pieces, tucking the inner curved edges of **D** beneath **C** as shown. Pin in place. Arrange the red/orange **D** appliqués around the **corner C** pieces in the same manner.

9 Next, arrange the **E** leaves on each side of each **D**, tucking the inner curved edges of **E** beneath **D**. Appliqué the **C, D** and **E** pieces in place using matching thread.

10 Position the **F** leaves on each side of the **B** stems, angling the leaves as shown; baste. Appliqué the **F** and **B** pieces using matching thread. Position **G** in the middle of each **A** flower; appliqué in place.

ASSEMBLY

11 Assemble the front of the baby quilt, the batting and the back as directed on page 109.

12 Outline-quilt the love apple, stem and leaf appliqués; also quilt inside the appliqués, following the lines on the templates.

13 Next, quilt the white background of the quilt. Using a pencil or chalk, draw a straight diagonal line connecting the opposite corners of the quilt. (Do not draw on top of the appliqués, just between them on the white background.) Quilt along the marked line, then work parallel lines of quilting to the left and right of this line, spacing the lines 1 inch apart. **Optional:** If you wish to create a cross-hatch design (not shown here), work quilting lines in the same manner in the opposite direction.

14 Bind the quilt with a separate green binding as directed on pages 110-111.

ASSEMBLY DIAGRAM

Lap Quilt

ABILITY LEVEL: ADVANCED

SIZE

Block: 9$^{1}/_{2}$ inches square;
4 blocks required
Finished quilt: 31 inches square

MATERIALS

◆ 1$^{5}/_{8}$ yards green print fabric
(includes fabric for back of quilt)
◆ $^{1}/_{4}$ yard gold print fabric (includes
fabric for binding)
◆ $^{1}/_{4}$ yard solid gold fabric
◆ $^{1}/_{4}$ yard brown print fabric
◆ $^{1}/_{8}$ yard rust fabric
◆ 31$^{1}/_{2}$ x 31$^{1}/_{2}$ inch piece of batting

CUTTING

Note: A $^{1}/_{4}$ inch seam allowance is
included in all measurements; templates
do not include a seam allowance. Full-
size templates can be found on page 119.

Quilt back: 1 piece, 31$^{1}/_{2}$ x 31$^{1}/_{2}$ inches,
green print fabric.
Sashing and Borders: From green print
fabric, cut 2 **E** strips, 4$^{1}/_{2}$ x 10 inches; 3 **J**
strips, 4$^{1}/_{2}$ x 23$^{1}/_{2}$ inches; 2 **K** strips 4$^{1}/_{2}$ x
31$^{1}/_{2}$ inches.
Binding: Cut 3 strips across the full width
of the gold print fabric, each 1$^{1}/_{2}$ inches
wide; stitch the strips together so that the
binding measures 3$^{3}/_{4}$ yards long.

Sunflower Blocks: (Number of pieces
for a single block are in parenthesis.)

Pattern Piece	Number of Pieces	
A	(8)	32 gold print
	(8)	32 solid gold
	(16)	64 rust
B	(8)	32 solid gold
C	(4)	16 green print
D	(1)	4 brown print

PIECING

1 Arrange the pieces for one Sunflower block on a flat surface, with the gold print **A** pieces surrounding the central **D** octagon. Position the rust **A** pieces as the points of the flower, and place the solid gold pieces around the outer edges of the patchwork. Sew the pieces together as directed on pages 34-35. Repeat for the other 3 blocks, arranging the colors in the same manner.

2 Arrange the blocks on a flat surface with the **E**, **J** and **K** sashing and border strips as shown in the **Assembly Diagram.**

3 Sew an **E** sashing strip between the pairs of blocks to make 2 vertical strips.

4 Sew the vertical strips to opposite sides of one **J** strip.

5 Sew a **J** strip to the top and bottom edges of the patchwork.

6 Sew a **K** strip to each side of the patchwork to complete the quilt top.

ASSEMBLY

7 Assemble the front of the lap quilt, the batting and the back as directed on page 109.

8 Outline-quilt each block. Quilt a second line 1/2 inch away from the outer edges of each block.

9 Trace the star and border patterns on pages 118-119; make a template for each design as directed on page 110.

10 Transfer the small star to the exact middle of the lap quilt.

11 Transfer the large star over the middle of the patchwork block, aligning the 4 large points of the star with the 4 corners of the block.

12 Transfer the border design all around the borders of the quilt. Then transfer a section of the border design to each of the sashing strips (**E** and **J**) starting the border design just beyond the edges of the star.

13 Quilt the marked designs. Quilt a meandering line within the quilted circle on each of the **D** pieces.

14 Finally, quilt 1/2 inch and 1 inch away from the outer edges of the quilt.

15 Bind the lap quilt with a separate gold binding as directed on pages 110-111.

ASSEMBLY DIAGRAM

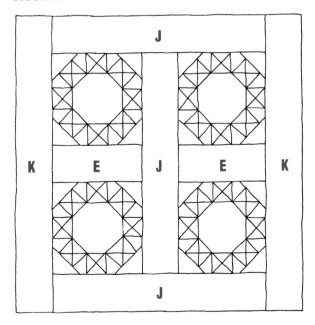

Tote Bag

ABILITY LEVEL:
INTERMEDIATE

Rainbow Schoolhouses

SIZE

Block: 9 inches square;
1 block required

Finished bag: Approximately 16 inches square

MATERIALS

◆ 1 yard black fabric (includes fabric for back of bag and straps)

◆ $^5/8$ yard solid red fabric (for lining)

◆ $^1/4$ yard red print fabric

◆ $^1/4$ yard (or large scrap) yellow fabric

◆ $^5/8$ yard plain fabric for quilting (this fabric will be hidden by the lining)

◆ 2 pieces of batting, each 20 x 18 inches

◆ 2 strips Vilene / iron-on interfacing, each $3^1/2$ x 28 inches

◆ $1^1/8$ yards red rickrack (optional)

CUTTING

Note: A $^1/4$ inch seam allowance is included in all measurements; templates do not include a seam allowance. Full-size templates can be found on pages 120-121.

W Strips: 4 strips, $1^1/2$ x $9^1/2$ inches, black fabric.

Back: 1 piece, 16 x 16 inches, black fabric.

Side Panels: 4 strips, $2^1/2$ x 16 inches, black fabric.

Bottom Panels: 2 strips, $2^1/2$ x 20 inches, black fabric.

Plain Fabric for Quilting: 2 pieces, each 20 x 18 inches, plain fabric.

Lining: 2 pieces, 20 x 18 inches, solid red fabric.

Straps: 2 strips, 3 x 28 inches, black fabric.

Schoolhouse Block:

Pattern Piece	Number of Pieces
A	1 black
B	2 red
C	2 black
D	1 red
E	1 black
E (R)	1 black
F	1 red
G	1 black
H	2 black

J	4 red
K	3 red
L	2 red, 2 black
M	1 red
N	2 red, 2 black
O	1 black
P	2 red
Q	1 red
Sashing	
R	4 black
S	32 yellow
T	4 yellow
W	4 black
X	8 black
Y	4 black

PIECING

1   Piece one Schoolhouse block and 4 **S-R-S** sashing strips as directed on pages 60-62.

2   Arrange the block on a flat surface with the sashing strips around it as shown in the **Front Assembly Diagram**. Sew the side sashing strips to each side of the block.

3   Sew a **T** square to each end of the remaining 2 sashing strips, then sew to the top and bottom edges of the block.

4   Construct an **S-X-S** unit by sewing an **S** triangle to each angled edge of an **X** triangle. Repeat 7 more times for a total of 8 **S-X-S** units

5   Sew an **S-X-S** unit to each end of the 4 **W** strips.

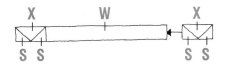

6   Sew 2 of the strips just made to each side of the patchwork block, matching seams carefully.

7   Sew a **Y** square to each end of the remaining 2 strips.

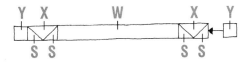

8   Sew the pieces just made to the top and bottom edges of the patchwork.

9   Sew a side panel to each side edge of the bag front.

10 Sew a side panel to opposite edges of the fabric for the back of the bag.

11 Sew the bottom panels to the bottom edges of the front and back pieces.

QUILTING

12 Assemble the front of the bag, the batting and the plain fabric for quilting as directed on page 109.

13 Quilt the patchwork following the **Quilting Diagram** on page 121. Outline-quilt the stars, then quilt in the ditch along the remaining seamlines. Quilt the flower and leaf design in the **R** sashing pieces; quilt the flower only in the middle of the **T** squares. **Optional:** Quilt the flower and leaf design on each side panel.

FRONT ASSEMBLY DIAGRAM

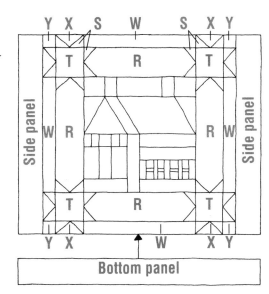

BACK ASSEMBLY DIAGRAM

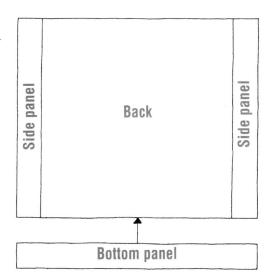

14 Assemble the back of the bag, the batting and the plain fabric for quilting.

15 Quilt the square back panel of the bag with horizontal and vertical lines, spaced 1 inch apart so that the lines criss-cross to form a checkerboard as shown in the illustration for step 23. Alternatively, you can quilt the design of your choice on the back. Also quilt in the ditch along the seamlines joining the back to the side and bottom panels. **Optional:** Quilt the flower and leaf design on each side panel.

ASSEMBLY

16 With right sides facing and raw edges even, pin the front of the bag to the back; stitch the pieces together making a ¼ inch seam, and backstitching securely at each end. Begin at one top edge, sewing down to the corner. Turn your stitching at the corner to sew the bottom panels together; at the opposite corner, continue sewing up to the top edge to finish.

17 Finger-press the seam along the bottom panel **open.** At one bottom corner, arrange the bag as shown to create a triangle at the corner. Sew across the triangle so that your stitching line

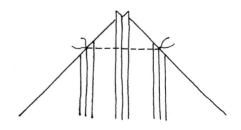

measures 4 inches from edge to edge (this will create a gusset across the bottom panels of the bag). Repeat for the other corner.

LINING

18 Place the lining pieces together with right sides facing, raw edges even and with the 18 inch edges at the sides. Stitch the lining pieces together as directed in step 16. Stitch gussets along the bottom edges as you did in step 17.

19 Fold and press the raw top edges of the lining ¼ inch to the wrong side; baste in place. Turn the lining right side out.

20 Fold the raw top edges of the bag ¼ inch to the wrong side and baste in place. The bag should be wrong side out.

21 Slip the lining over the bag, matching the seams at the side edges. Pin the lining to the bag all around the top, matching the folded edges. Slip-stitch in place using matching thread. Remove the basting stitches. Turn the bag to the right side, arranging the lining neatly inside the bag. Catch-stitch the lining to the bottom of the bag at the corners to hold it firmly in place.

FINISHING

21 For the straps, place one strip of Vilene / iron-on interfacing on the wrong side of each fabric strip; press together. Fold each strap in half lengthwise and stitch the long edges and one short edge together. Using a tube-turner, turn each

strap to the right side and press. Fold the raw ends inside and slip-stitch the folded edges together.

23 Pin the ends of the straps inside the bag near the top edge to determine the position you find most comfortable. Adjust the straps as necessary, then sew the ends of the straps firmly inside the bag.

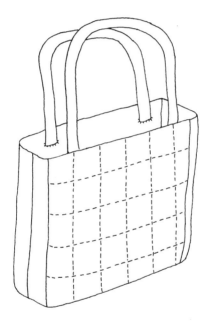

24 For a decorative finish, pin rickrack around the inside of the bag near the top edge and slip-stitch in place.

25 For a crisp finish at the side edges of the bag, pinch the fabrics together along each of the side seams and topstitch from top to bottom.

Framed Block

ABILITY LEVEL: ALL LEVELS

Summer Berries

SIZE

Depends on size of quilt block chosen; 1 block required

MATERIALS

◆ see materials list for the block you have chosen; you will probably only need large scraps of each color listed

◆ about ¼ yard coordinating fabric to border the block

◆ plain fabric to back the block for quilting

◆ batting cut to size of block plus 6 inches

CUTTING

Note: A ¼ inch seam allowance is included in all measurements; templates do not include a seam allowance. Full-size templates for Summer Berries can be found on page 121.

Borders: From the coordinating fabric, cut 4 strips, each 3 inches wide times the length of the block plus 6 inches.

Back (for quilting): cut plain fabric to size of block plus 6 inches.

PIECING OR APPLIQUÉ

1 Piece or appliqué one of the blocks in this book in the colors and fabrics of your choice, following the directions given with that design.

2 Sew a border centered along each side of the block.

3 Sew a border to the top and bottom edges of the block in the same manner. Miter the corners as directed on page 109.

ASSEMBLY

4 Assemble the block, the batting and the plain fabric for the back as directed on page 109.

5 Quilt the block as directed in the individual instructions. Outline-quilt the seams of the borders.

6 Take the quilted block to a framer to have it professionally framed, or buy the necessary supplies to frame it yourself. If you are going to protect the textile with glass, make sure that the glass does not actually touch the fabric.

ASSEMBLY DIAGRAM

Cushion

ABILITY LEVEL: BEGINNER

Birds in the Air

SIZE
Block: 6 inches square;
4 blocks required
Finished cushion: 16 inches square

MATERIALS
◆ ³/8 yard light fabric (includes fabric for piping)
◆ ¹/2 yard dark blue fabric (includes fabric for back of cushion)
◆ scraps of three other coordinating fabrics
◆ 16¹/2 inch piece of batting
◆ 16¹/2 inch square of plain fabric for quilting the cushion front (this fabric will be hidden inside)
◆ 2 yards cotton piping cord
◆ 12 inch dark blue zipper
◆ 16 inch square pillow form

CUTTING
Note: A ¹/4 inch seam allowance is included in all measurements; templates do not include a seam allowance. Full-size templates can be found on page 125.
Back of Cushion: From dark blue

fabric, cut one piece, 15 x 16¹/2 inches; one piece, 2¹/2 x 16¹/2 inches.
Borders: From dark blue fabric, cut 2 **C** strips 2¹/2 x 12¹/2 inches; 2 **D** strips 2¹/2 x 16¹/2 inches.
Piping: Cut 2 strips across the full width of the light fabric, each 1¹/2 inches wide; stitch strips together so piping strip measures 2 yards long.

Birds in the Air Blocks:

Pattern Piece	Number of Pieces
A	12 light
	6 dark blue
	6 coordinating
	6 coordinating
	6 coordinating
B	4 light

PIECING

1 Piece 4 Birds in the Air blocks as directed on pages 50-51.

2 Arrange the blocks on a flat surface with the pieced triangles all in the same position. Sew 2 pairs of blocks together; press the seam allowances in opposite directions.

3 Stitch the pairs together, matching seams carefully in the middle. Press.

4 Stitch a **C** border to the top and bottom edges of the patchwork; press the seam allowances toward **C**.

5 To complete the cushion front, stitch a **D** border to each side edge of the patchwork; press the seam allowances toward **D**.

ASSEMBLY DIAGRAM

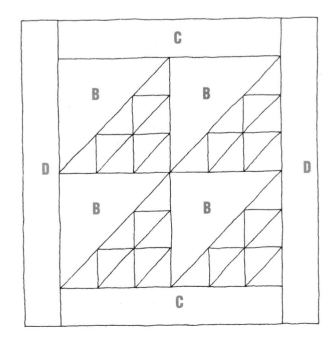

ASSEMBLY

6 Assemble the cushion front, batting and the plain fabric for quilting as directed on page 109.

7 Quilt the patchwork portion of the cushion front in horizontal and vertical lines, following the lines of the patchwork, and continuing the stitching across the unpieced **B** triangles.

8 Next quilt diagonal lines across the patchwork, following the lines of the patchwork and continuing the stitching across the unpieced **B** triangles.

9 Quilt $1/4$ inch away from the inner edge of the border all around; repeat $1/2$ inch away from the outer border.

PIPING

10 Sew the piping to the cushion front following the instructions on page 111.

CUSHION BACK

11 With right sides facing, raw edges even and making a $1/2$ inch seam, sew the long edges of the 2 rectangles together, using regular stitching for $2^{1}/4$ inches, changing to basting for 12 inches and changing back to regular stitches for the last $2^{1}/4$ inches. Press the seam allowance open.

12 Insert the zipper into the basted portion of the cushion back as directed on page 111.

FINISHING

13 With right sides facing and raw edges even, pin the cushion back and quilted front together all around, sandwiching the piping in between. (Leave the zipper partially open to facilitate turning the cushion cover to the right side after sewing the back and front together.)

14 Using the zipper foot on your sewing machine, stitch the pieces together all around, sewing as close to the piping cord as possible.

15 Turn to the right side to check the stitching. If all is well, turn the cushion cover inside out again and sew another line of stitching, $1/8$ inch away from the raw edges. Clip off each of the corners. Zigzag-stitch the raw edges all around.

16 Turn to the right side and insert a pillow form, adjusting the corners to fit into each corner of the cushion cover. Close the zipper.

PROJECT

Table Centerpiece

Rose Wreath

ABILITY LEVEL: ADVANCED

SIZE

Centerpiece: 35$\frac{1}{2}$ inches in diameter

MATERIALS

◆ 2 yards plaid fabric (includes fabric for back)

◆ 1 yard green fabric (includes fabric for bias binding)

◆ $\frac{3}{8}$ yard red fabric

◆ scrap gold fabric

◆ 36 x 36 inch piece of batting

◆ pencil, string (about 38 inches long) and push pin for marking circle

CUTTING

Note: A $\frac{1}{4}$ inch seam allowance is included in all measurements; templates do not include a seam allowance. Full-size templates can be found on page 125.

Background Square and Back: 2 pieces, 36 x 36 inches, plaid fabric.

Bias strip: From green fabric, cut one 29 inch square. Following the instructions for bias binding on page 108, cut 1$\frac{1}{4}$ inch wide bias strips and sew together to measure 4$\frac{1}{2}$ yards long. Cut one strip, 43 inches long for the **A** piece; prepare this strip for appliqué as directed on page 109. The remainder of the bias strip will be used for binding the outer edges of the centerpiece.

Rose Wreath Block:

Pattern Pieces	Number of Pieces
A	1 green
B	4 red
C	8 green
D	12 green
D (R)	12 green
E	16 red
F	8 green
G	4 gold

– 96 –

APPLIQUÉ

1 Appliqué one Rose Wreath block in the center of the background square as directed on pages 54-56. Do not remove the basting that indicates the center point of the square.

2 Make a compass by tying one end of the string around a pencil, and the other end around a push pin; the string should measure 36 inches when taut. Place the appliquéd background square on a flat surface with some newspaper or cardboard under the exact middle. Push the pin into the center of the background square (where the basting lines cross) and into the paper or cardboard you have laid beneath the project. Have someone hold the pin firmly in place while you swing the pencil around to mark a 36 inch circle on the fabric.

3 Cut out the fabric along the marked pencil line. Use this fabric as a pattern to cut out the batting and the fabric for the back.

ASSEMBLY

4 Assemble the appliquéd front, the batting and the back for quilting as directed on page 109.

5 Outline-quilt each of the appliqués.

6 Follow the design of the plaid fabric to quilt the background. You can work as much quilting as you wish, provided that you do not leave an area larger than 2 inches unquilted.

7 Mark 2 circular lines for quilting near the outer edge of the centerpiece. The first line should be 3 inches away from the outer edge; the second line should be 6 inches away from the outer edge. Do not mark on top of the appliqués. Quilt along the marked lines.

8 Bind the project with a separate green bias binding as directed on pages 110-111, allowing only a narrow edge of the binding to show on the right side.

ASSEMBLY DIAGRAM

Wall Hanging

ABILITY LEVEL: ADVANCED

Oak Leaf and Reel

SIZE

Block: 16^1/$_2$ inches square;
1 block required
Finished wall hanging: 32^1/$_2$ inches
square

MATERIALS

◆ 2^1/$_8$ yards white fabric (includes
fabric for back of wall hanging and
sleeve)

◆ ^{3}/$_4$ yard green fabric (includes fabric
for binding)

◆ ^{1}/$_2$ yard pink fabric

◆ 33 x 33 inch piece of batting

CUTTING

Note: A ^{1}/$_4$ inch seam allowance is
included in all measurements; templates
do not include a seam allowance. Full-
size templates can be found on pages
116-117.

Back: 33 x 33 inches, white fabric.

Background square: 17 x 17 inches,
white fabric.

Borders: 2 **L** strips 8^1/$_2$ x 17 inches,
white fabric; 2 **M** strips 8^1/$_2$ x 33 inches,
white fabric.

Binding: Cut 3 strips across the full
width of the green fabric, each 1^1/$_2$ inches
wide; stitch strips together so binding
measures 4 yards long.

Sleeve: 7^1/$_2$ x 33 inches, white fabric.

Oak Leaf and Reel Block:

Pattern Piece	Number of Pieces
A	4 green
B	1 pink
Border:	
C	8 green
D	8 pink
E	4 pink
F	4 pink
G	4 pink
H	4 pink

APPLIQUÉ

1 Appliqué one Oak Leaf and Reel
block as directed on pages 78-79.

2 Sew an **L** border to the top and
bottom edges of the block.

3 Sew an **M** border to each side of the
block.

4 Arrange the **C** crescents on the
border pieces, fitting 2 along each side of

the quilt. Adjust the space between the crescents as necessary to fit them evenly along the borders. Pin in place.

5 Prepare pieces **D, E, F, G** and **H** for appliqué. These pieces will comprise the tasselled bows between the **C** crescents on the border; refer to the illustrations on page 80 for placement.

6 Arrange a **D, E** and **F** appliqué in each of the 4 corners of the quilt. Position **D** over the space between the crescents in one corner. Position **E** and **F** beneath **D**, tucking the ends underneath **D**. Appliqué in place using matching thread. Repeat for the other 3 corners of the quilt.

7 Arrange a **D, G** and **H** appliqué along each of the 4 sides of the quilt. Position **D** over the space between the crescents as you did in Step 6. Position **G** and **H** beneath **D**, tucking the ends underneath **D**. Appliqué in place using matching thread. Repeat for the other 3 tassels.

8 Appliqué the **C** crescents to the borders using matching thread.

ASSEMBLY

9 Assemble the front of the wall hanging, the batting and the back as directed on page 109.

10 Outline-quilt each of the appliqués.

11 Quilt the area between the leaves with 3 curved lines to echo the curves of the **A** crescents. Then quilt the remainder of the background with a series of curved lines to echo the curves of the **C** crescents.

12 Bind the wall hanging with a green binding as directed on pages 110-111.

SLEEVE

13 Prepare the sleeve by folding and pressing the **short** raw ends under ⅛ inch and again anothe ⅛ inch; stitch in place.

14 With right sides facing and raw edges even, sew the long edges of the sleeve together, making a tube. Press the seam allowance open.

15 Turn the tube to the right side. Press the tube so that the seam allowance is centered along one side, making a sharp crease-line at the top edge of the tube. For the bottom edge of the tube, press a crease so that the right side of the sleeve

(the side without the seam allowance) is ¼ inch bigger than the side with the seam. This will allow some 'give' when the hanging device is inserted through the sleeve; in this way, the front of the wall hanging will not bulge outward at the top when it is hung – the sleeve will do the bulging!

16 Pin the sleeve to the back of the wall hanging, so that the top crease is aligned with the edge of the binding. Slip-stitch the top and bottom edges in place, allowing every third stitch to penetrate through the batting and the front. Make sure that the right side of the sleeve 'balloons' slightly outward.

17 Insert a wooden batten or metal rod through the sleeve for hanging.

ASSEMBLY DIAGRAM

Table Runner

Evergreen

ABILITY LEVEL: BEGINNER

SIZE

Block: 9 inches square;
3 blocks required
Finished runner: 13¼ x 38½ inches

MATERIALS

◆ ⅞ yard red plaid fabric (includes fabric for back of runner)
◆ ⅜ yard solid red fabric
◆ ⅜ yard green print fabric (includes fabric for binding)
◆ ¼ yard white print fabric
◆ 15 x 43 inch piece of batting

CUTTING

Note: A ¼ inch seam allowance is included in all measurements; templates do not include a seam allowance. Full-

size templates can be found on page 124.

Side T Triangles: Cut 1 square from the red plaid fabric, 14 x 14 inches. Cut the square diagonally into 4 quarters to make 4 triangles.

Corner U Triangles: Cut 2 squares from the red plaid fabric, each 7 ¼ x 7¼ inches. Cut each square diagonally in half to make 4 corner triangles.

Back of Runner: 13$\frac{1}{4}$ x 39 inches, red plaid fabric.

Binding: Cut 3 strips across the full width of the green fabric, each 1$\frac{1}{2}$ inches wide; stitch strips together so binding measures 3$\frac{1}{4}$ yards long.

Evergreen Block:

Pattern Piece	Number of Pieces
A	2 green, 1 white
B	3 red
B(R)	3 red
C	4 green, 2 white
D	3 red
D(R)	3 red
E	2 green, 1 white
F	3 red
F(R)	3 red
G	2 green, 1 white
H	3 red
H(R)	3 red
J	3 red
J(R)	3 red
K	3 brown
L	3 red
L(R)	3 red
M	6 red

PIECING

1 Piece 3 Evergreen blocks, one with a white tree and 2 with green trees as directed on pages 68-69.

2 Arrange the 3 blocks on a flat surface with the side and corner triangles as shown in the **Assembly Diagram**.

3 Sew a **T** triangle to opposite sides of the block with the white tree for the middle of the runner.

4 For the green block on the left, sew a **T** side triangle to the top right edge, then sew a **U** corner triangle to the 2 left-hand edges of the block.

5 For the green block on the right, sew a **T** side triangle to the lower left edge, then sew a **U** corner triangle to the 2 right-hand edges of the block.

6 Sew the pieced strips together, matching the seams carefully where the corners of the blocks meet to complete the top of the runner. Press carefully.

ASSEMBLY

7 Assemble the front of the table runner, the batting and the red plaid fabric for the back of the table runner as directed on page 109.

8 Quilt $\frac{1}{4}$ inch away from the seams on each patchwork piece comprising the Evergreen blocks.

9 Quilt in the ditch along the outer edges of the blocks. You may find that the area where the blocks meet may bulge out slightly; if this is the case, work a few stab stitches exactly through the points where the seams intersect.

10 Follow the design of the red plaid fabric to quilt the side and corner triangles. You can work as much quilting as you wish, provided that you do not leave an area larger than 2 inches unquilted.

11 Bind the table runner with a separate green binding as directed on pages 110-111, mitering each of the corners neatly.

ASSEMBLY DIAGRAM

Christmas Stocking

Double Irish Chain

ABILITY LEVEL: BEGINNER

SIZE

Block: 10 inches square;
3 blocks required
Finished stocking: About 22^1/$_2$ inches long

MATERIALS

◆ ^{3}/$_4$ yard green fabric (includes fabric for back of stocking)

◆ ^{1}/$_8$ yard red fabric

◆ ^{1}/$_4$ yard gold fabric

◆ ^{3}/$_4$ yard fabric for quilting (this fabric will be inside the stocking)

◆ ^{1}/$_4$ yard coordinating fabric for binding

◆ 2 pieces, 20^1/$_2$ x 23 inches, batting

◆ embroidery floss in a contrasting color

◆ Templates (measurements include seam allowance):

    E: 6^1/$_2$ x 10^1/$_2$ inches

    H: 2^1/$_2$ x 2^1/$_2$ inches square

    J: 2^1/$_2$ x 6^1/$_2$ inches

CUTTING

Note: If you are a beginner, it would probably be best to use templates to cut out the individual pieces. However, if you are proficient with a rotary cutter, or confident about your cutting, you can cut the pieces for this stocking by using a rotary cutter and ruler (or by marking the fabrics with a pencil and ruler and cutting with scissors). Cut all your strips 2^1/$_2$ inches wide; you can then cut these strips into squares (for the **H** pieces) or into 6^1/$_2$ inch lengths for the **J** pieces. All measurements include a ^{1}/$_4$ inch seam allowance. Templates given for tracing do not include a seam allowance; full-size templates for the border pieces can be found on page 125.

Stocking back: One piece, 20^1/$_2$ x 23 inches.

Bias binding: From the coordinating fabric, cut one 9^1/$_2$ inch square. Following the instructions for bias binding on page 108, cut 1^1/$_2$ inch wide bias strips and sew together to measure 2^3/$_4$ yards long.

Blocks: (There are no pieces **A-D**; these are used to make the quilt.)

Pattern Pieces	Number of Pieces
E	1 gold
F	3 gold
G	8 red
	2 gold
H	18 red
	28 green
	8 gold
J	2 gold

PIECING

1 Cut out all the required pieces for the stocking front and arrange on a flat surface following the **Assembly Diagram** and the photograph on the facing page for color placement.

2 Write the appropriate name across the **E** piece and embroider the name in outline or chain stitch using 3 strands of embroidery floss in the needle.

3 Sew the **H, E** and **J** pieces together in horizontal rows, starting at the top of the design and working down to the bottom.

4 Sew the rows together, matching seams carefully at the corners.

5 For the diamond border, stitch a **G** triangle to opposite sides of 3 **F** squares as shown; stitch these diagonally-shaped strips to each other, matching the seam allowances carefully where the points of the **F** squares meet. Stitch a red and a gold **G** triangle to each end of the strip to square the ends. This will create a top border strip that is 10½ inches long.

6 Stitch the border to the top edge to complete the stocking front.

7 Following the **Assembly Diagram**, carefully trim the **H** pieces at the inner edge of the stocking and at the heel and toe to create nicely rounded curves.

8 Use the patchwork front of the stocking to cut a piece in reverse for the stocking back.

9 Assemble the front of the stocking, the batting and the fabric for quilting, as directed on page 109.

10 Quilt diagonal lines across the squares, following the points where the patchwork pieces intersect. If you wish, you can quilt diagonal lines in the opposite direction to create a cross-hatch pattern.

11 Quilt the back of the stocking in a cross-hatch pattern composed of intersecting diagonal lines.

12 Bind the top edges of the stocking front and back with separate bindings as directed on page 110.

13 Place the stocking front and back together, carefully matching the side and bottom edges. Stitch the pieces together from one top edge, down the stocking, around the heel and toe and up to the opposite top edge.

14 Bind the raw edges of the stocking with the bias binding, easing the binding carefully around the curves. Fold the raw edges under at the ends and stitch in place invisibly.

15 Make a hanging loop with the remaining bias binding; fold the ends under to enclose the raw edges then stitch the ends of the loop inside the stocking at the back edge.

ASSEMBLY DIAGRAM

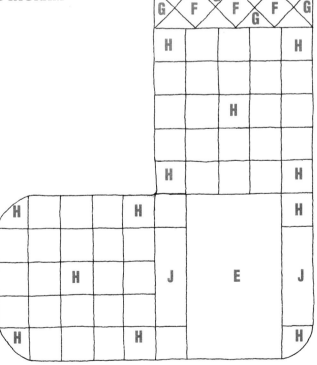

Basic Techniques

This section covers the quiltmaking techniques that you will need to know in order to make the seasonal quilts and projects featured in this book.

MATERIALS AND SUPPLIES

◆ **Needles:** Use Sharps for hand-sewing and Betweens for quilting.

◆ **Thimble:** Essential for quilting; optional for hand-sewing.

◆ **Thread:** Use No. 50 cotton thread for hand-sewing and No. 40 thread for machine sewing in a color that will blend with your fabrics. Use 100% cotton thread for quilting.

◆ **Pins:** Choose smooth fine dressmaker's pins with glass or plastic heads.

◆ **Seam Ripper:** Necessary for removing machine-sewn stitches.

◆ **Steam Iron:** Pressing is an essential aspect of quiltmaking; steam will help set the seams and remove wrinkles.

◆ **Dressmaker's Shears:** Extremely sharp for cutting fabric only.

◆ **Embroidery Scissors:** For clipping into seam allowances or cutting thread ends.

◆ **Paper Scissors:** For cutting pattern pieces and plastic templates.

◆ **Quilting Hoop:** A wooden hoop, around 14 inches in diameter will help keep an even tension on your work as you quilt.

SUPPLIES FOR MAKING TEMPLATES

◆ **Pencils:** Sharp lead pencils and white or silver dressmaker's pencils.

◆ **Dressmaker's Ruler:** Clear plastic ruler marked with horizontal and vertical lines.

◆ **Utility Knife:** For cutting cardboard or plastic when making templates.

◆ **Metal-Edge Ruler:** Run the blade of the utility knife against the metal edge of this ruler to cut out templates from cardboard or plastic.

◆ **Medium-Weight Cardboard:** Recycle medium-weight cardboard to make into templates.

◆ **Graph Paper:** For drawing patchwork designs and templates.

◆ **Spray Glue:** For making templates.

FABRICS

See pages 8-11 for a discussion on how to select fabrics and how to create special antique effects. Pre-wash all of your fabrics before cutting them out. Clip into the selvages to prevent uneven shrinkage, then put like-colors in the washing machine with a small amount of fabric softener if you wish; you needn't use detergent since new fabrics shouldn't be dirty. Wash the fabrics in hot water, then hang to dry; drying in a machine may twist long lengths of fabric off grain. Press with a steam-iron to remove the wrinkles, striving to keep the grain straight as you iron.

If, after washing, you are unsure about whether a fabric is colorfast, soak it in a solution of three parts cold water to one part white vinegar, then rinse the fabric until the water runs clear. Wash the fabric again with a small tester piece of white fabric. If the tester cloth shows any discoloration or other sign of the dye bleeding, discard the fabric.

CUTTING THE FABRICS

The fabric yardages that are given with each set of instructions assume careful measuring and cutting. If you wish to add a margin of safety by buying extra fabric, you can always use the leftover fabric in a future project. As a general rule, when cutting out the pieces, first cut the fabrics for the quilt back, then the borders, background blocks and binding. Cut the smaller patchwork or appliqué pieces from what remains.

All of the measurements given for cutting the larger pieces such as the quilt back, borders and binding, include a ¼ inch seam allowance. None of the templates include a seam allowance (to save space in the book), so be sure to add a ¼ inch seam allowance to each piece.

MAKING AND USING TEMPLATES

Templates are durable pattern pieces made of cardboard or plastic, used to cut out the pieces comprising a patchwork or appliqué design. Accuracy is extremely important when making templates; measure carefully and use sharp pencils for making templates and for marking outlines on fabric.

To make templates, trace the pattern pieces for the design you have chosen, labelling each piece with the appropriate letter and pattern name. Cut out the paper pieces, spray the wrong side with glue, and press onto medium-weight cardboard. Place the cardboard on a cutting mat or thick sheaf of newspaper and use a utility knife and a metal-edge ruler to cut out the shape. If you are making a quilt with many pieces, make several templates for each piece and discard when they become worn out. For complicated or curved designs, mark notches in the edges of the templates to aid in matching the pieces when you sew them together.

If you are going to hand-sew patchwork or if you are going to appliqué, do not add a seam allowance to the templates, as the seamlines for these pieces must be marked on the fabric. When you position the templates for hand-sewing or appliqué on the fabric, leave at least ½ inch between the pieces to accommodate the seam allowances.

For machine-sewn patchwork, the seam lines do not need to be drawn on the fabric, so add a ¼ inch seam allowance around all the edges of each template before cutting them out.

Always mark the longest edge of a patchwork piece along the straight grain of the fabric; if possible, leave a mutual cutting edge between adjacent pieces to conserve fabric.

ROTARY CUTTING

You will need a rotary cutter with a large blade, a rotary ruler (a clear plastic ruler marked with straight and angled lines) and a self-healing cutting mat (available in quilt shops and art supply stores).

To prepare the fabric, fold it in half on the straight grain with the selvages matching; steam-press the layers together. Fold in half again matching the first fold to the selvages and creating four layers; steam-press again. Carefully pick up the pressed fabric without unfolding it and place it on the cutting mat. Position the rotary ruler on the fabric, aligning one of the grid lines on the ruler with the pressed and folded edge of the fabric (the one opposite the selvage edge). Use your left hand to press down firmly on the rotary ruler, placing your little finger just off the edge of the ruler to prevent shifting. Run the blade of the rotary cutter along the edge of the ruler, keeping the blade perpendicular to the fabric; this will trim off and straighten any ragged edges; see **Diagram 1**. Shift your left hand carefully up the ruler as you cut. Always push the blade away from you.

Diagram 1

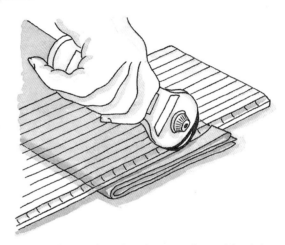

To cut strips of fabric, first decide upon the width of the strips you require, then add ½ inch for seam allowances. Position the ruler on the fabric so that your cutting edge is the required distance from the straightened edge of the fabric; cut in the same manner you used to trim the ragged edges. To cut squares, cut a strip ½ inch wider than the desired finished size of the square. Cut off the selvages, then place the ruler over the strip and cut a piece to the same width as the strip to create four perfect squares.

PATCHWORK

In patchwork, where you are joining many little pieces together, it is important that seams are sewn accurately. Always sew pieces together with the right sides of the fabric facing one another and the raw edges even. Seam allowances in patchwork are ¼ inch wide, and must be marked on the patches when hand sewing.

BASIC TECHNIQUES

HAND SEWING

Hand-sewn stitches must be evenly spaced but not too crowded. Seams are sewn from corner to corner along the lines marked on the patches. Hold the fabric so that you can see the sewing lines on each side. Make a backstitch at the end of the seam and work evenly spaced running stitches along the marked seam lines. Make a backstitch at the opposite corner. To join rows by hand, hold the sewn pieces together with the right sides facing, matching the seams, and inserting pins where necessary to secure the pieces. At each seam, knot or backstitch the thread, then insert the needle through the seam allowance to the other side so that you are leaving the seam allowances free. Knot or backstitch again before sewing the rest of the seam.

Basting is a temporary stitch used to secure pieces together before sewing or quilting them. Use a long length of light colored thread that will contrast with the surrounding fabric for easy removal. Make running stitches about 1/2 inch long, spaced about 1/2 inch apart.

MACHINE-SEWING

For machine-sewn patchwork, you'll need a basic machine in good working order. Use a standard straight stitch set at a length of 10-12 stitches per inch. Because the sewing lines are not marked as in hand piecing, you should use the edge of your presser foot or a marked line on the throat plate of your sewing machine as a stitching guide; test whichever device you use to ensure that the seam allowance is exactly 1/4 inch. Stitch the pieces together at an even speed, guiding the fabric with your hand. If you are using pins, remove the pins before you sew over them, as sewing over pins will dull your needle. If you are joining lots of patches, sew them together in a chain to save time and thread as shown in **Diagram 2.** To secure machine-sewn stitches, you can backstitch using the reverse lever on your sewing machine. Alternatively, you can shorten the length

of your stitches, making them very tiny where you wish the knot to be. It is not necessary to backstitch at each edge of each patch – only where you know that a seam or edge will be under stress, or when insetting. Press the seam allowances to one side, preferably toward the darker fabric. If you cannot avoid pressing toward a light fabric, trim the seam allowance so that the dark fabric does not show through to the right side.

To join rows of patches by machine, make sure that the seam allowances are pressed in opposite directions to reduce bulk and to make matching the seam easier. Pin the pieces together directly through the stitching, and to the right and left of the seam to prevent the pieces from shifting.

HOW TO INSET

A number of the patchwork designs in this book require insetting, which is when a patchwork piece is sewn into the angled area formed by the joining of two other pieces. Following **Diagram 3,** join the pieces forming the angle by sewing them together; end your stitching exactly 1/4 inch from the edge to be inset .

Diagram 3

Following **Diagram 4** on the facing page, pin the piece to be inset to one edge of the angle and stitch from the inside to the outer edge in the direction of the arrow.

Diagram 2

Diagram 4

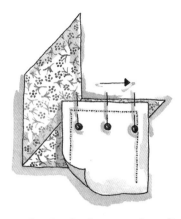

Following **Diagram 5,** pin the inset to the adjacent angle. Stitch from the inside to the outside edge following the arrow, and begin your stitching exactly where the other line of stitching began (at the seam). Open out the fabrics and carefully steam-press.

Diagram 5

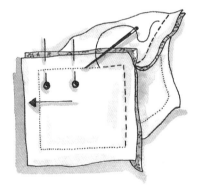

HOW TO SEW CURVES

The secret to sewing curved patches successfully is to cut the pieces with the curves on the bias; then the pieces are easy to manipulate and fit together. Mark the seam allowances and the

Diagram 6

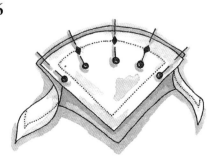

notches (for matching) on the wrong side of the fabric pieces. Pin the pieces together, matching the notches and the side edges first. Match and pin any other notches, then continue pinning, easing and smoothing the pieces to fit; see **Diagram 6**. Sew the pieces together by hand or machine, securing the beginning and end of the seam with knots or backstitches, then open out and steam-press carefully.

APPLIQUÉ

The technique of appliqué is done by placing (or applying) one piece of fabric on top of another and then sewing it in place with invisible stitches. To prepare pieces for appliqué, first mark the templates on the wrong side of the fabric, making sure to leave 1/2 inch between the pieces for seam allowances. Cut out the pieces, adding a 1/4 inch seam allowance around each one. Clip into the curved edges of the appliqués perpendicular to the marked outline of the piece as shown in **Diagram 7**; do not clip beyond the marked line. Make extra clips along deep curves for ease in turning. Straight edges need not be clipped. Then, turn the raw edges of the appliqués 1/4 inch to the wrong side and hand-baste in place. Steam press the folded edges carefully.

Diagram 7

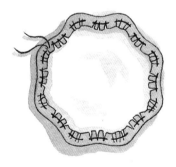

Narrow corners, such as the tips of leaves, can be very tricky. For perfect corners, follow **Diagram 8** on the following page. First clip into the seam allowance 1/4 inch below the tip and trim the seam allowance to 1/8 inch, then trim off the point 1/8 inch above the marked turning line as shown in **8a**. Fold the point down to the wrong side as shown in **8b**. Fold one edge of the appliqué 1/4 inch to the wrong side as shown in **8c**, then fold the second edge to the wrong side, overlapping the first edge at the top and bottom as shown in **8d.** Baste the edges in place and press carefully.

Diagram 8

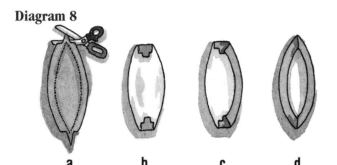

| a | b | c | d |

For complicated designs, mark the outlines of the major pieces on the right side of the background fabric. Pin, then baste the appliqués in position. When you are satisfied with the arrangement, slip-stitch the appliqués to the background, using matching thread and making tiny invisible slip-stitches; see **Diagram 9**.

Diagram 9

Making Bias Strips and Bindings

To make bias strips either for appliquéd vines or for binding a quilt, cut a square of fabric to the required size on the straight grain of the fabric. (**Note:** When a long length of bias is required, you may be instructed to cut more than one square of fabric. Treat each square separately, following the instructions to make the bias, then join the ends of the bias strips to make the required length.)

Following **Diagram 10,** cut the fabric in half diagonally, then with the right sides facing, stitch the edges indicated by arrows together, making a $1/4$ inch seam.

Press the seam allowance open. Following the individual instructions for the required width, mark parallel lines across the seamed fabric as shown in **Diagram 11**. Take care not to stretch the fabric as you mark it.

Diagram 10

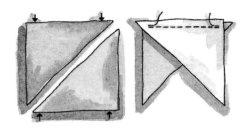

Diagram 11

Following **Diagram 12,** pin the diagonal edges of the marked fabric together with right sides facing, offsetting the edges so that the top edge of the fabric aligns with the first marked line. Match the marked lines as you pin the edges together. Then stitch together, making a $1/4$ inch seam.

Diagram 12

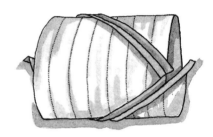

Press the seam allowance open then, beginning at the top edge, cut the fabric along the marked lines in one continuous spiral as shown in **Diagram 13**. Take care in handling the bias strip as it will stretch easily.

Diagram 13

To prepare a bias vine or stem for appliqué, carefully fold the bias strip in half lengthwise with the *wrong* sides facing; stitch the long raw edges together making a $1/4$ inch seam; trim the seam to a scant $1/8$ inch. Gently press the strip with the raw edges of the seam centered on one side, taking great care not to stretch the strip out of shape. You can now easily manipulate the bias strip and shape it into graceful curves by steam-pressing and gentle modeling with your fingers. When appliquéing the strip to a base fabric, position the strip with the seamed side down.

HOW TO MITER CORNERS

Stitch the border strips to the quilt top with right sides facing, making a $1/4$ inch seam; press the strips to the right side, allowing the excess border fabric to extend evenly beyond each edge of the quilt top. Following **Diagram 14,** fold one border strip back on itself, forming a $45°$ angle; press and pin in place. Then stitch the folded edge of the border to its counterpart either by hand from the right side, or by machine from the wrong side. Press carefully, then trim both seam allowances to $1/2$ inch.

Diagram 14

ASSEMBLING A QUILT

A quilt is composed of three layers: the quilt top, the batting and the back. The quilt tops in this book are either patchwork or appliquéd. For the quilt back, which is generally in a fabric that matches the quilt front, only one central seam is usually required to achieve the correct width; however if the quilt is quite large, you may need to sew two strips of fabric to either side of a central panel. The batting can be cotton, wool or polyester. You will need a large, clean flat surface on which to assemble the pieces.

First, steam-press the quilt top and quilt back very carefully. This will be the last time these fabrics can be pressed, so do a good job. Remove any frayed edges or threads from the wrong side of the fabrics. If there are any bulky areas, clip away excess fabric carefully from the wrong side.

Place the quilt back, wrong side up, on the large flat surface; if you can, use masking tape to secure the edges to the surface and keep the back taut. Next, place the batting on top of the quilt back, centering it between all the side edges. Finally, place the quilt top, right side up, over the batting, again smoothing it carefully in place. Baste the layers together horizontally, vertically and diagonally, working from the middle of the quilt out to the edges. If the quilt will be moved around a lot or if you are planning to quilt it using a hoop, add extra rows of concentric basting to hold the three layers together securely; see **Diagram 15.**

Diagram 15

QUILTING

Quilting stitches are simply running stitches which pass through all three layers of a quilt, anchoring them together firmly, and at the same time, adding some texture to the work which often brings it to life.

Cut a 18 inch length of 100% cotton quilting thread. Make a knot in the end of the thread, then pass the thread through the top of the quilt, pulling it so that the knot pops through the top layer and becomes buried in the batting. With one hand below the quilt to guide the needle upward, begin working a series of running stitches through all three layers of the quilt.

Basic Techniques

Try to make the stitches the same length on the front and back. If you use the nail of one of your fingers beneath the quilt, you will prevent yourself from being pricked as you guide the needle back up to the surface, or you can wear a thimble on the finger below the quilt. Make three or four stitches at a time, rocking the needle from the surface to the quilt back and then to the surface again; pull the stitches through. If the quilt is in a hoop or frame, you can pull quite firmly, which will provide greater definition to your quilting stitches. When you reach the end of the length of thread, make a knot close to the surface of the quilt, then make a backstitch through the quilt top and batting only, pulling the knot beneath the surface and burying it in the batting.

To use the quilting designs given in this book, trace the full-size quilting pattern; make a complete pattern if it is given quarter-size, and make a cardboard template of the whole shape. If there are interior or complicated design lines, cut channels in the template for ease in marking. Place the template on the quilt top and mark around the edges and along the channels using a sharp pencil – silver pencils work well as the lines seem to disappear as you quilt.

If you are instructed to quilt *in-the-ditch*, you must stitch as close to a seam as possible on the side opposite where the seam allowances have been pressed. If you are quilting along a seam where the position of the seam allowances alternate, just make a small stitch across the intersection and alternate your quilting line too; see **Diagram 16**.

Adding a Separate Binding

The binding is the finishing touch that determines the overall appearance of a quilt, so it is important that the edges lie smoothly. It is best to make your own binding so that you are certain of the quality of the fabric and so that it matches the rest of the quilt. Cut $1\frac{1}{2}$ inch-wide strips across the entire width on the straight grain of the fabric chosen for the binding. Refer to the Cutting section in the individual instructions for the amount of binding you need to cut. Sew the strips together; press the seam allowances open. Press the binding in half lengthwise with wrong sides facing one another. Then press one long edge of the binding to the center crease, again with wrong sides facing. Fold one end of the binding $\frac{1}{2}$ inch to the wrong side and place along one side edge of the quilt top with right sides facing and raw edges even. Stitch the binding to the quilt making a $\frac{1}{4}$ inch seam.

As you approach the first corner, shorten your stitch length. When the needle is exactly $\frac{1}{4}$ inch from the corner, stop stitching, leaving the needle in the corner point. Raise the presser foot and pivot the quilt on the needle to prepare to sew the next edge. Adjust the binding so that the raw edge is parallel to the next edge of the quilt. Allow a small tuck to form in the binding as shown in **Diagram 17**; do not catch this tuck in the stitching, as it will be used to miter the corner. Lower the presser foot and continue stitching with small stitches for about $\frac{1}{2}$ inch. Adjust the stitch length to normal and continue stitching to the next corner. Sew each corner in the same way.

Diagram 16

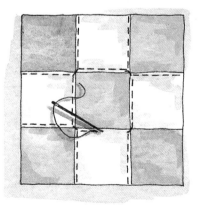

Diagram 17

When you reach the starting point, allow the binding to overlap the beginning fold by ½ inch as shown in **Diagram 18**; trim away any excess binding. Wrap the folded pressed edge of the binding over to the back, overlapping the stitching line; pin in place. Slip-stitch the binding to the quilt back using matching thread. Use a pin to adjust the tucks at each corner into a miter; slip-stitch in place.

Diagram 18

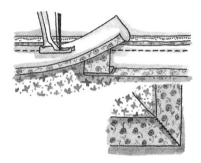

SIGNING THE QUILT

Always sign and date your quilts. Embroider your name and the date on a small piece of fabric either in cross-stitch or outline stitch. Or, you can write or type your name on the fabric with indelible ink. Hem all the edges of the fabric label, then stitch to the back of the quilt using matching thread. Alternatively, you can quilt or embroider your name and the date on the front of the quilt, making your signature and the date part of the overall design.

PROJECTS

The following techniques are used to construct the cushion covers in this book.

PIPING

Cut the piping strip to the length given in the Cutting section for the cushion cover you are making. Place the cotton piping cord on the wrong side of the piping fabric along the middle of the strip. Fold the fabric in half lengthwise with wrong sides facing, enclosing the piping cord. Using a zipper foot on the sewing machine, stitch close to the cord; trim the seam allowance to ¼ inch.

Starting in the middle of one side edge, pin the piping to the right side of the cushion front with the raw edges even. To ease the piping around each corner, clip into the seam allowance to the stitching line. Continue pinning the piping in place until you reach the starting point. Overlap the beginning of the piping by 1 inch, then cut off any excess. Remove 1 inch of stitching from the starting point of the piping, push back the excess fabric and trim away only the cord so that the beginning and end of the cord are flush as shown in **Diagram 19**. Now straighten out the excess fabric and finger-press the raw edge ½ inch to the wrong side (inside) by running your finger over the fold a few times. Slip the beginning of the piping inside the end so that the excess fabric covers all raw edges; pin in place. Using the zipper foot on your sewing machine, stitch the piping to the cushion front all around, curving the stitching gently around the corners.

Diagram 19

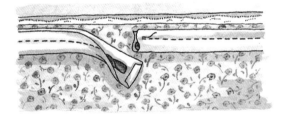

INSERTING A ZIPPER

Insert the zipper into the basted portion of the cushion back. Place the zipper, face down, over the basted seam, centering the teeth of the zipper exactly over the stitching of the seam. Pin in place. Hand-baste the zipper in place all around, stitching as close to the teeth of the zipper as is comfortable. Remove the pins. Using a zipper foot on the sewing machine, and sewing from the right side of the cushion back, stitch the zipper in place all around. Stitch about ¼ inch away from the seam. Work an extra row or two of stitching at each end of the zipper for extra strength. Remove the hand basting stitches. Then, using a seam ripper, carefully remove the machine basting stitches within the stitched portion of the zipper. Open and close the zipper to test it; remove any little threads that remain in the seam. ◆

Templates and Quilting Patterns

The templates and quilting patterns on the following pages have been grouped together by design. Refer to the chart below to find the page(s) on which the individual patterns appear. To save space, some of the patterns overlap, but you can differentiate between the pieces by looking for the identifying letter inside a balloon along one of the edges of each shape. Make a separate tracing for each pattern piece; label each one with the appropriate letter and grainline.

Some of the patterns are larger than the pages of this book. To make the pieces easier to trace, they have been split where they cross the middle of the book. When you are tracing the pieces, first trace the piece on the left-hand page, including the dot / dash lines, then line up your tracing with the dot / dash lines and the edge of the piece on the right-hand page to draw the rest of the pattern. Alternatively, the pieces have been drawn as half-or quarter patterns. When preparing the templates, first complete the half- or quarter-pattern before making the shape in cardboard or plastic as directed on page 105.

Note: The letter **I** is not used to label the template pieces.

All **asymmetrical** patchwork pieces are drawn in **reverse** so that when you mark the shapes on the wrong side of the fabric, the pieces will be facing the right way.

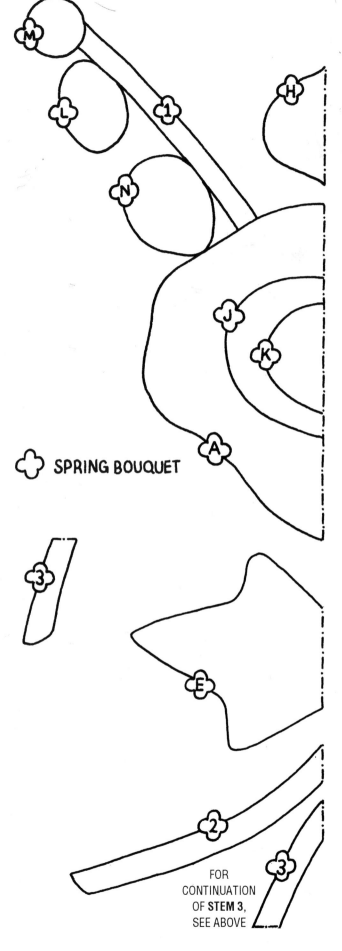

SPRING BOUQUET

FOR CONTINUATION OF **STEM 3**, SEE ABOVE

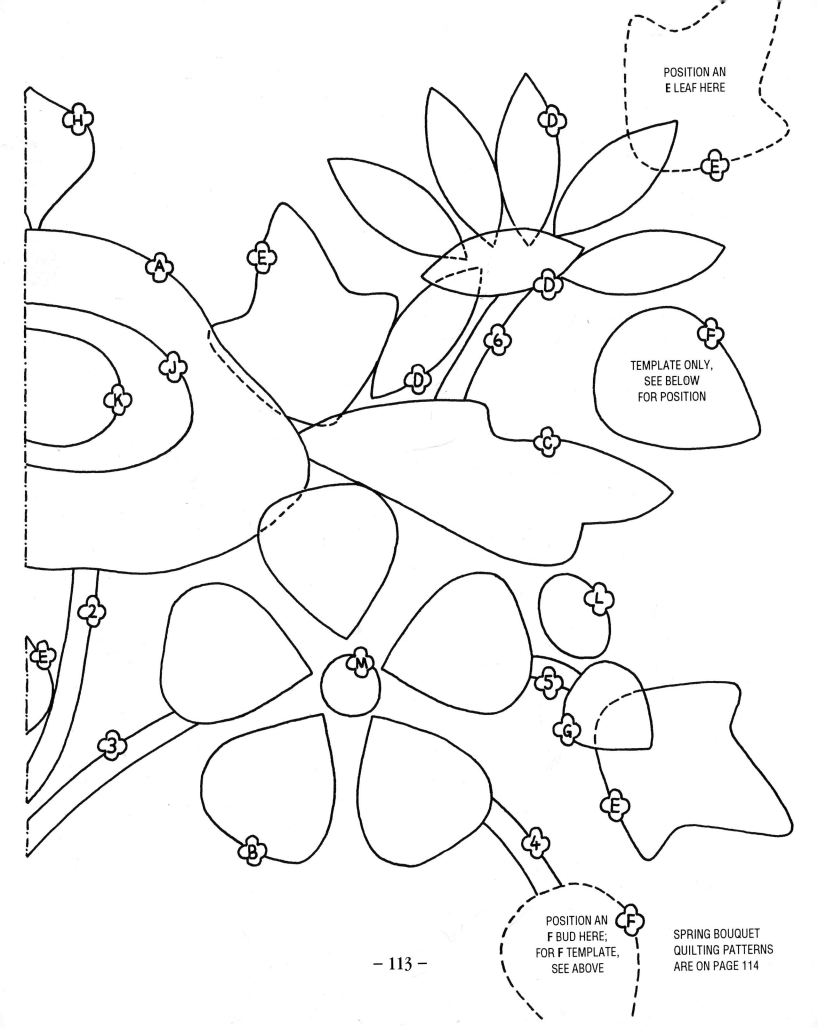

POSITION AN
E LEAF HERE

TEMPLATE ONLY,
SEE BELOW
FOR POSITION

POSITION AN
F BUD HERE;
FOR F TEMPLATE,
SEE ABOVE

SPRING BOUQUET
QUILTING PATTERNS
ARE ON PAGE 114

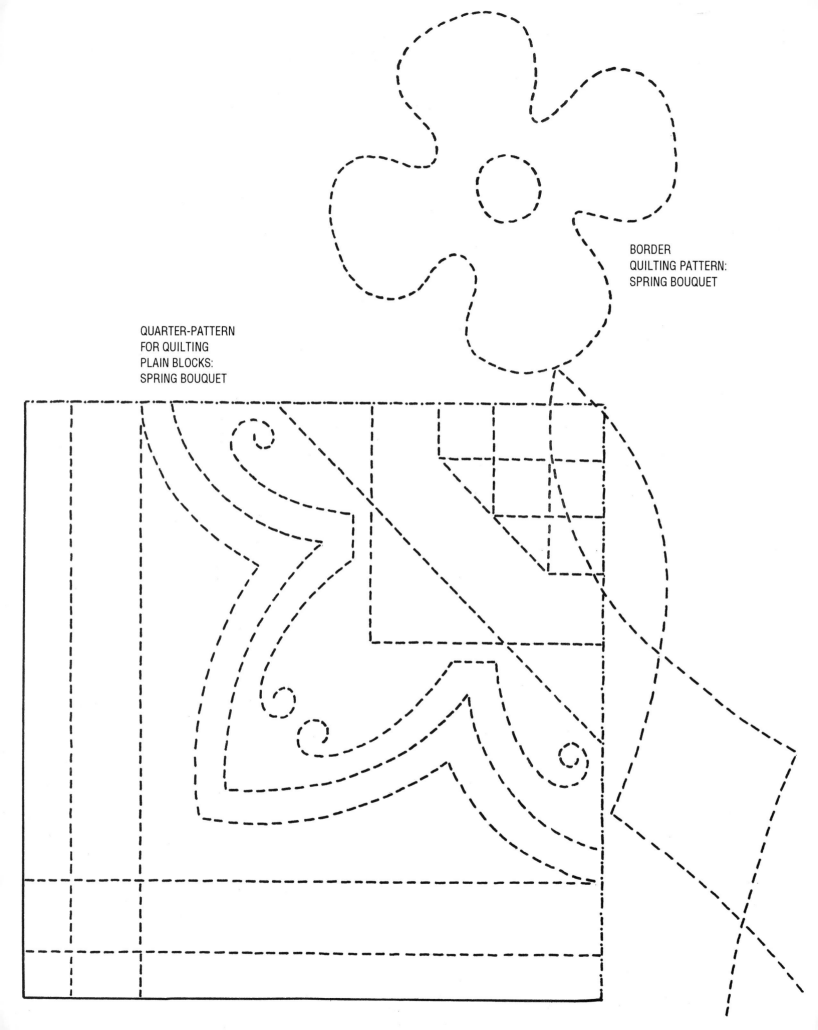

BORDER
QUILTING PATTERN:
SPRING BOUQUET

QUARTER-PATTERN
FOR QUILTING
PLAIN BLOCKS:
SPRING BOUQUET

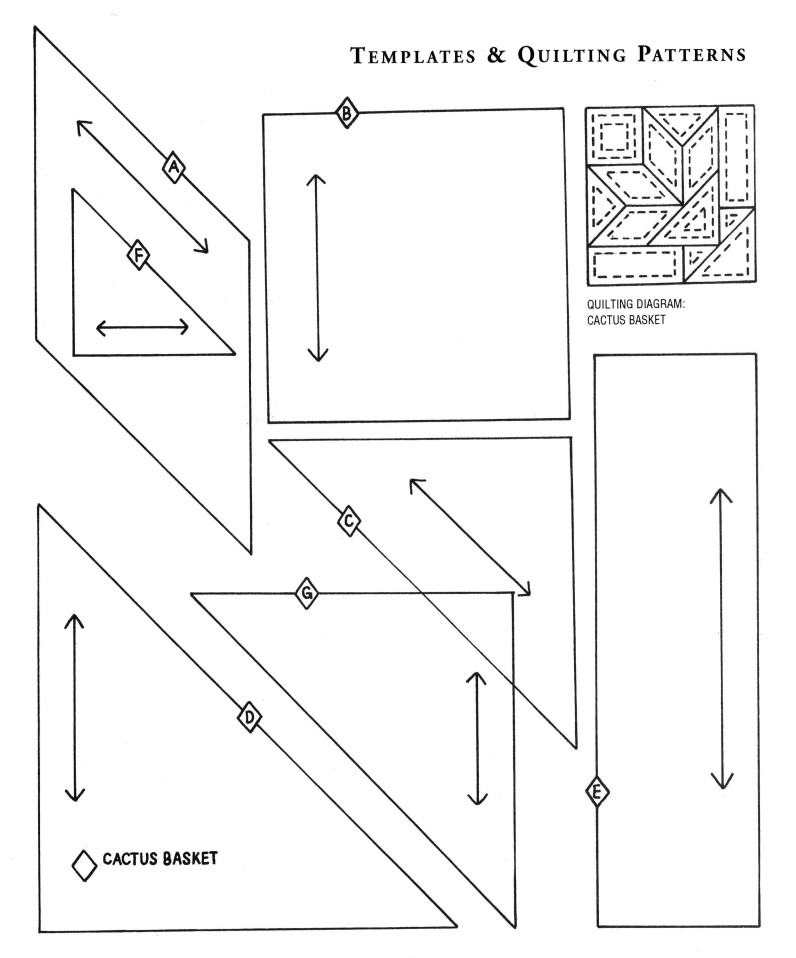

TEMPLATES & QUILTING PATTERNS

A

F

B

C

G

D

E

QUILTING DIAGRAM:
CACTUS BASKET

◇ CACTUS BASKET

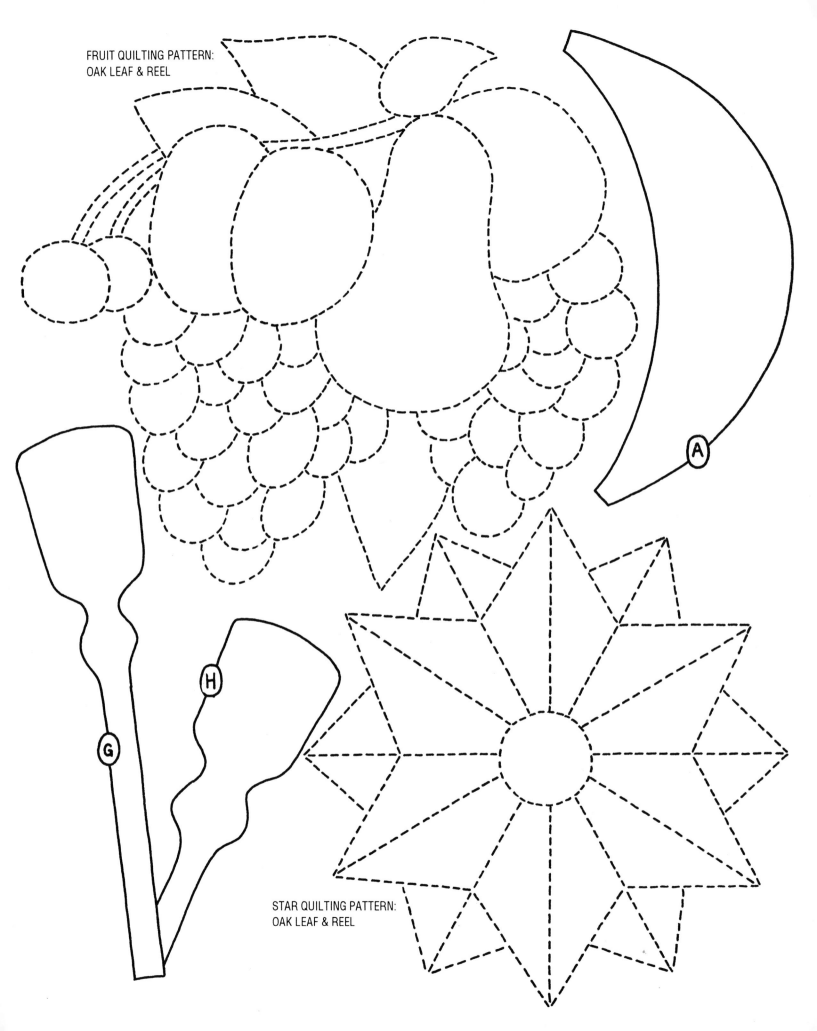

FRUIT QUILTING PATTERN:
OAK LEAF & REEL

STAR QUILTING PATTERN:
OAK LEAF & REEL

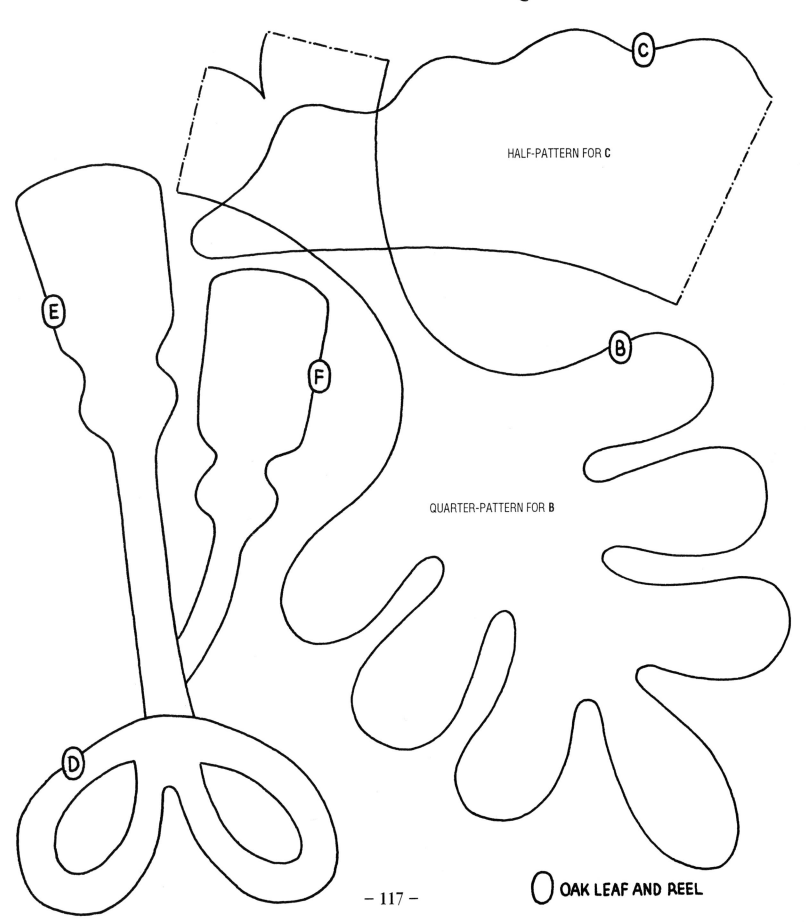

HALF-PATTERN FOR C

QUARTER-PATTERN FOR B

OAK LEAF AND REEL

TEMPLATES & QUILTING PATTERNS

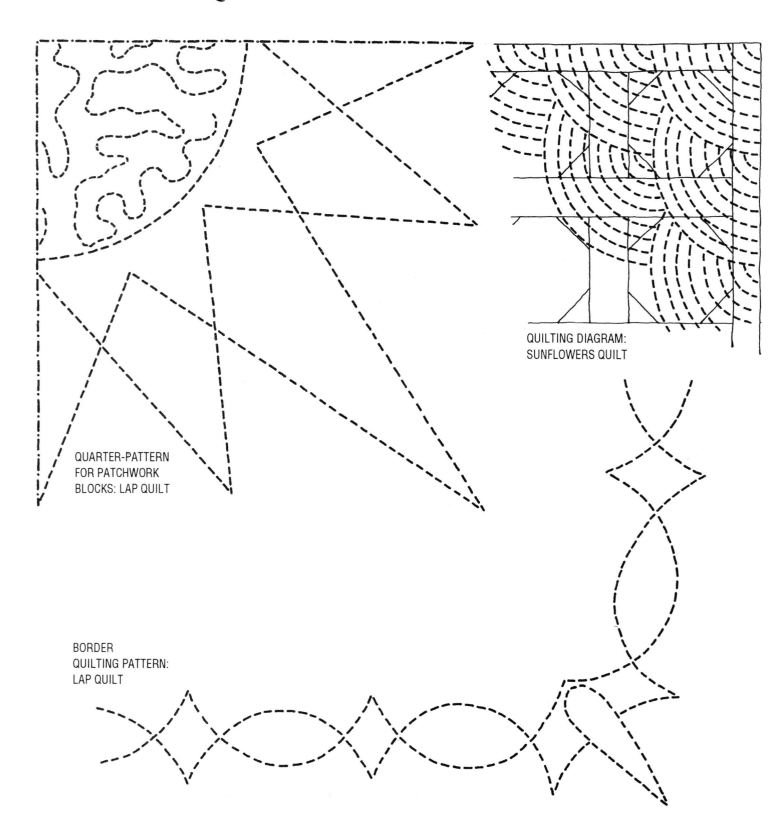

QUARTER-PATTERN
FOR PATCHWORK
BLOCKS: LAP QUILT

QUILTING DIAGRAM:
SUNFLOWERS QUILT

BORDER
QUILTING PATTERN:
LAP QUILT

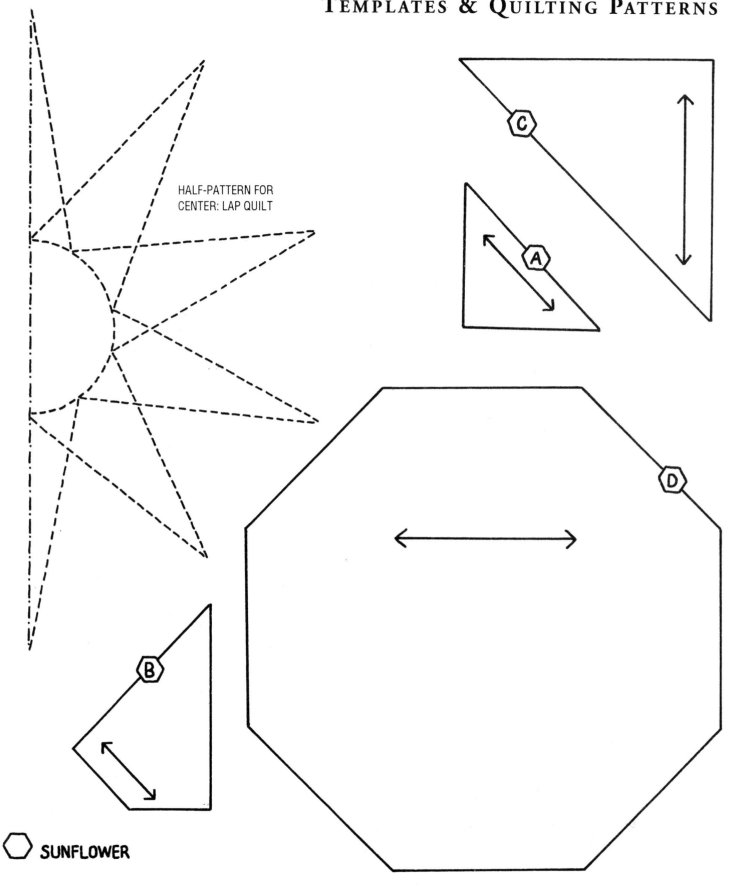

HALF-PATTERN FOR
CENTER: LAP QUILT

C

A

D

B

SUNFLOWER

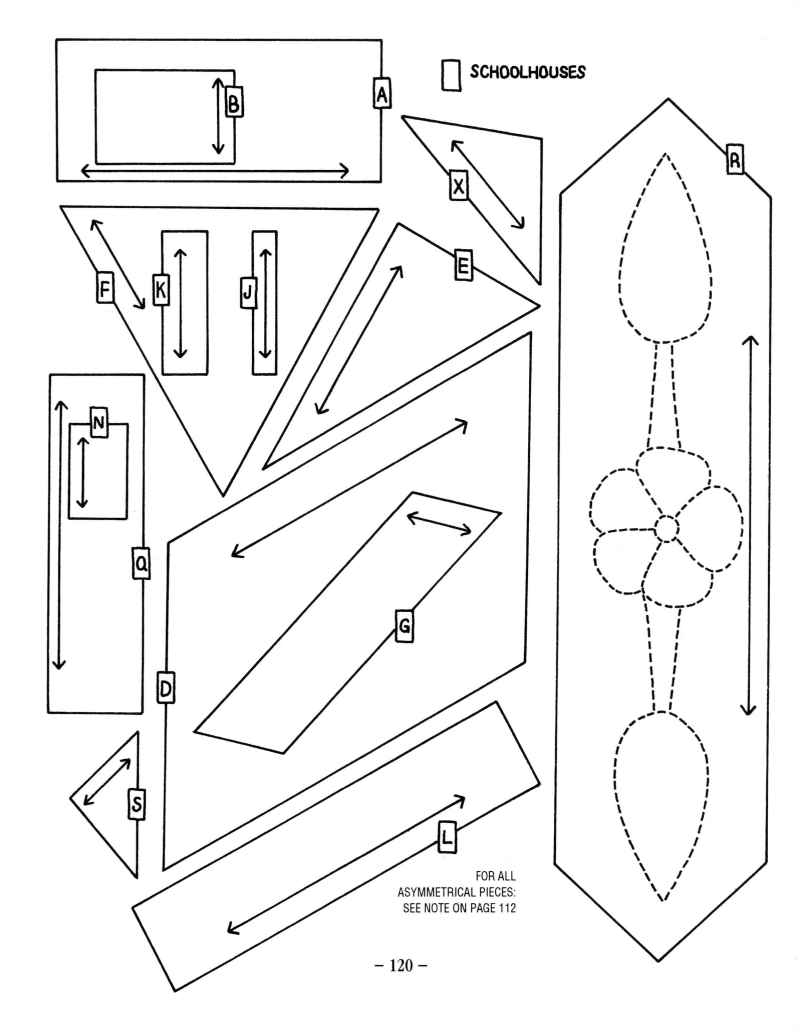

SCHOOLHOUSES

FOR ALL
ASYMMETRICAL PIECES:
SEE NOTE ON PAGE 112

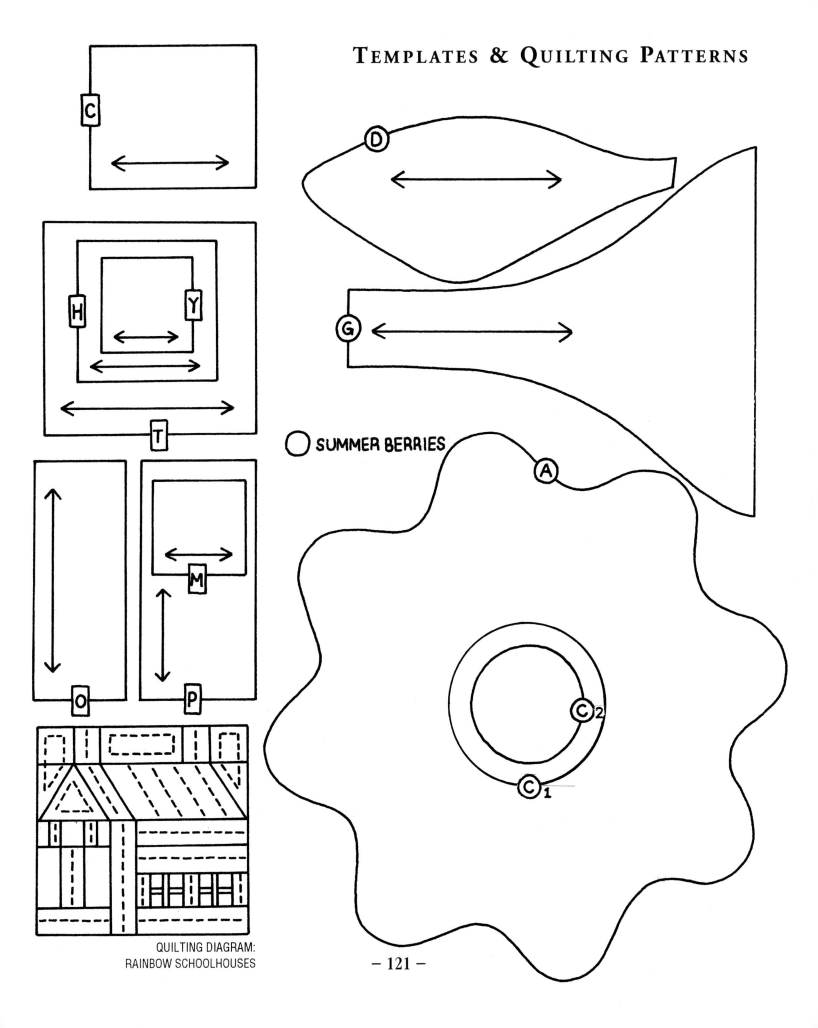

TEMPLATES & QUILTING PATTERNS

C

D

H   Y

T

G

O   M   P

SUMMER BERRIES

A

C₂

C₁

QUILTING DIAGRAM:
RAINBOW SCHOOLHOUSES

– 121 –

TEMPLATES & QUILTING PATTERNS

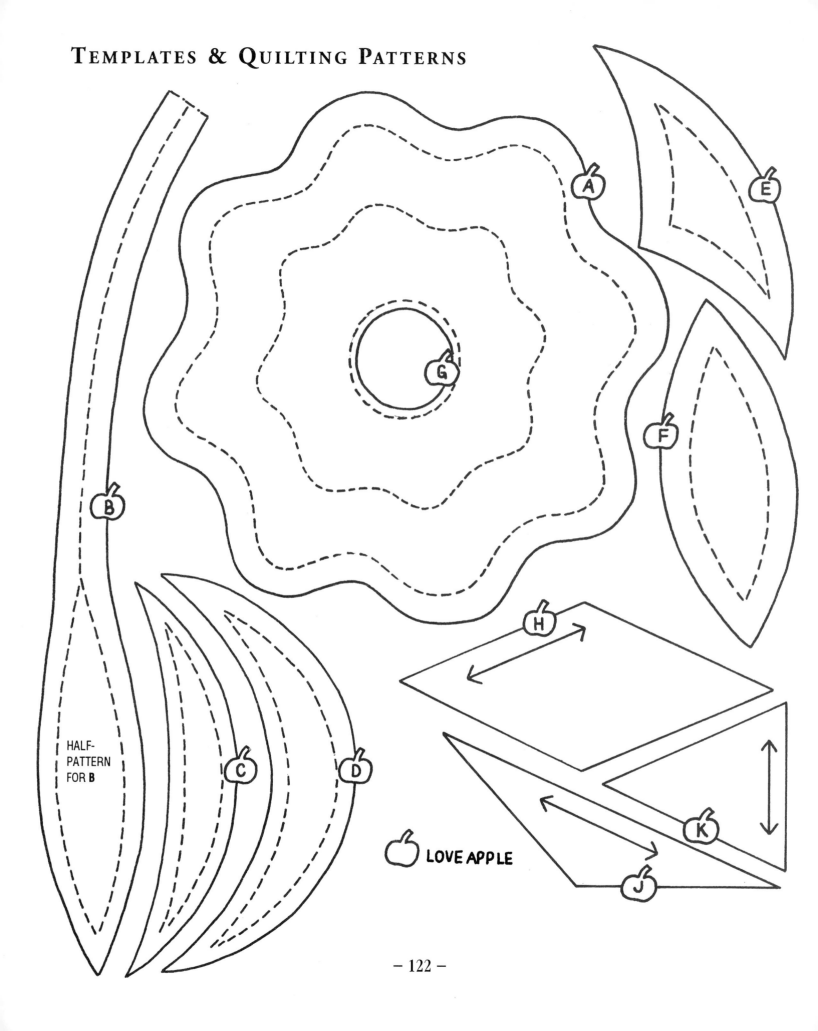

HALF-PATTERN FOR **B**

LOVE APPLE

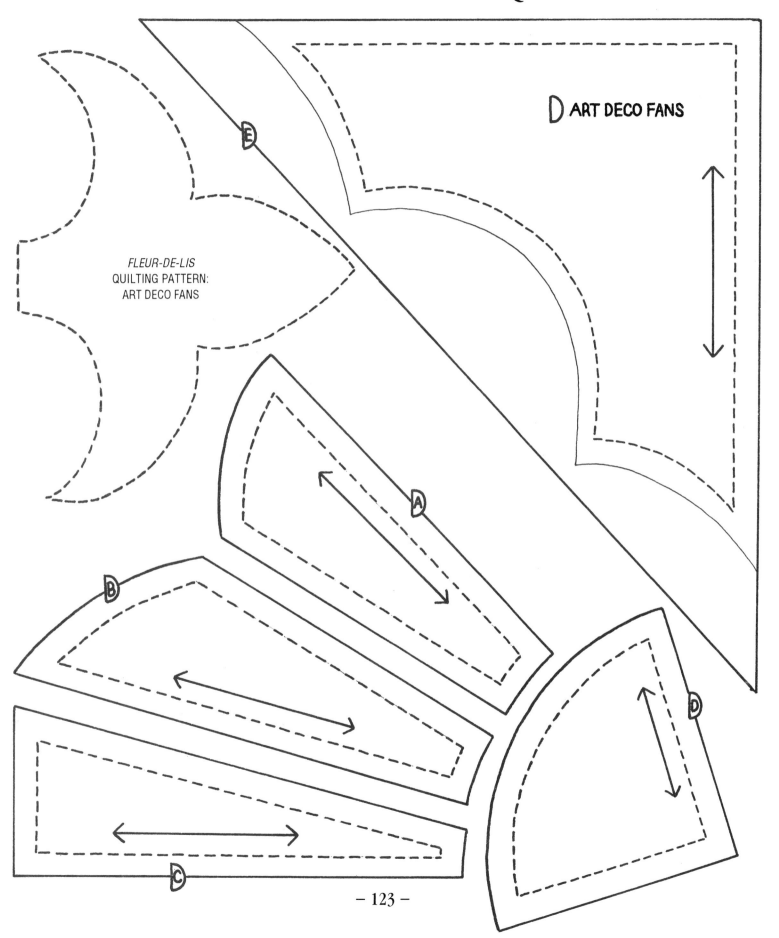

D ART DECO FANS

FLEUR-DE-LIS
QUILTING PATTERN:
ART DECO FANS

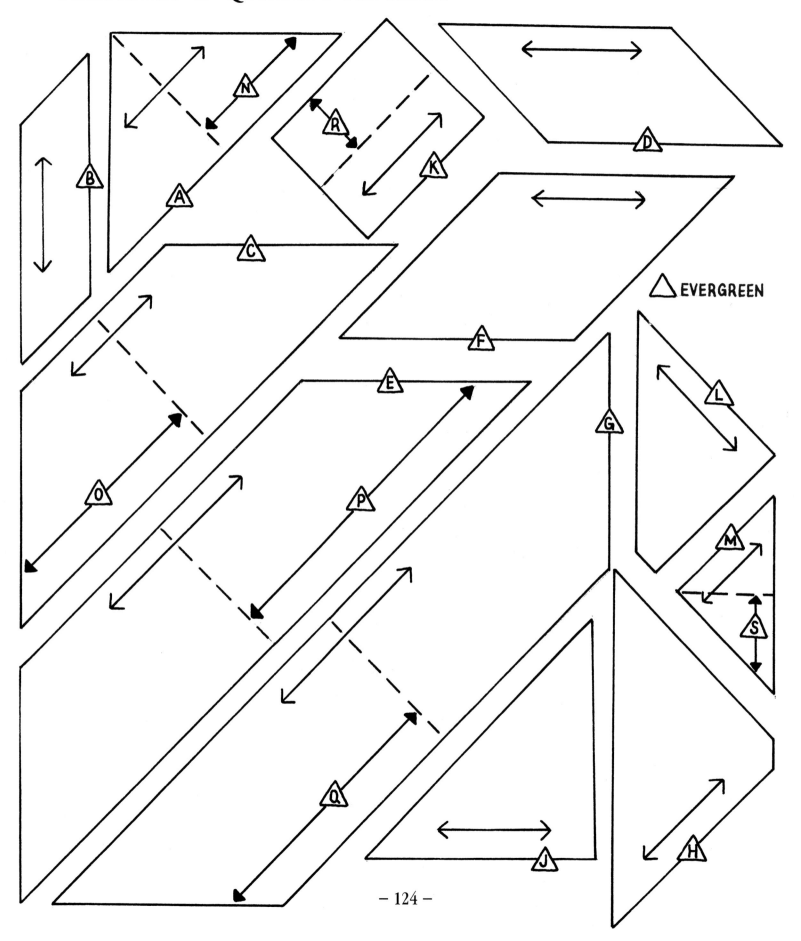

EVERGREEN

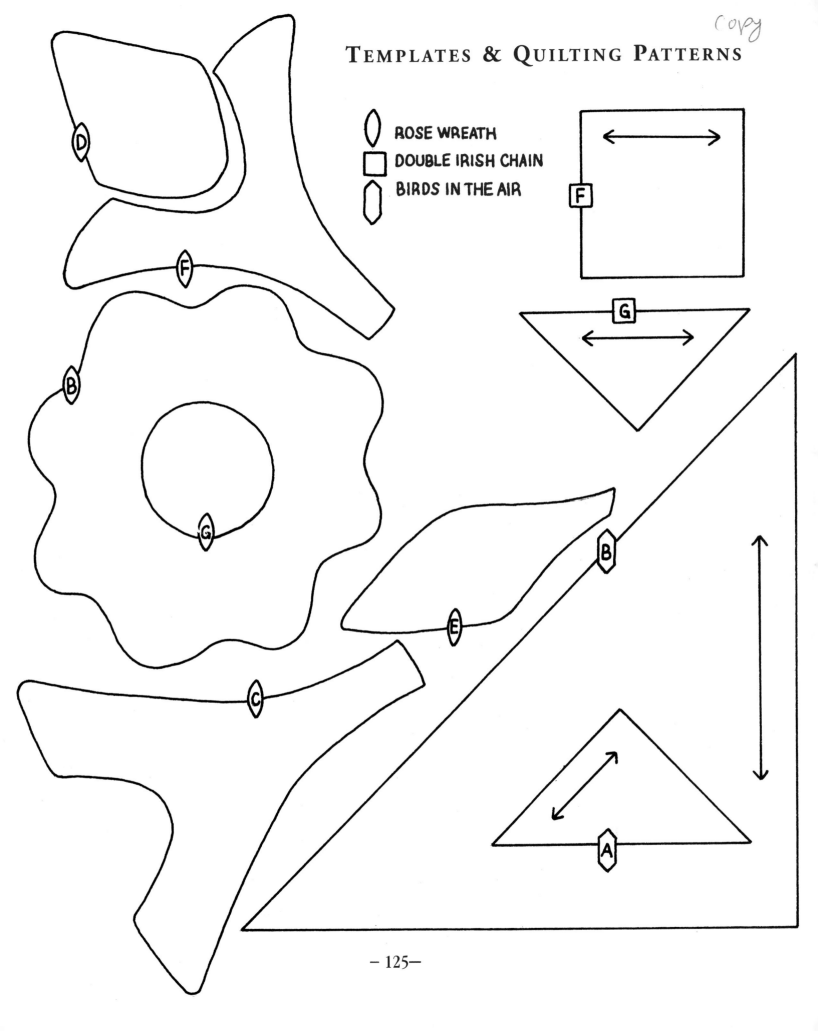

TEMPLATES & QUILTING PATTERNS

ROSE WREATH

DOUBLE IRISH CHAIN

BIRDS IN THE AIR

METRIC EQUIVALENCY CHART

MM – Millemetres   CM – Centimetres

Inches to Millimetres and Centimetres

INCHES	MM	CM	INCHES	CM	INCHES	CM
1/8	3	0.3	9	22.9	30	76.2
1/4	6	0.6	10	25.4	31	78.7
3/8	10	1.0	11	27.9	32	81.3
1/2	13	1.3	12	30.5	33	83.8
5/8	16	1.6	13	33.0	34	86.4
3/4	19	1.9	14	35.6	35	88.9
7/8	22	2.2	15	38.1	36	91.4
1	25	2.5	16	40.6	37	94.0
1 1/4	32	3.2	17	43.2	38	96.5
1 1/2	38	3.8	18	45.7	39	99.1
1 3/4	44	4.4	19	48.3	40	101.6
2	51	5.1	20	50.8	41	104.1
2 1/2	64	6.4	21	53.3	42	106.7
3	76	7.6	22	55.9	43	109.2
3 1/2	89	8.9	23	58.4	44	111.8
4	102	10.2	24	61.0	45	114.3
4 1/2	114	11.4	25	63.6	46	116.8
5	127	12.7	26	66.0	47	119.4
6	152	15.2	27	68.6	48	121.9
7	178	17.8	28	71.1	49	124.6
8	203	20.3	29	73.7	50	127.0

Yards to Metres

YARDS	METRES	YARDS	METRES	YARDS	METRES	YARDS	METRES	YARDS	METRES
1/8	0.11	2 1/8	1.94	4 1/8	3.77	6 1/8	5.60	8 1/8	7.43
1/4	0.23	2 1/4	2.06	4 1/4	3.89	6 1/4	5.72	8 1/4	7.54
3/8	0.34	2 3/8	2.17	4 3/8	4.00	6 3/8	5.83	8 3/8	7.66
1/2	0.46	2 1/2	2.29	4 1/2	4.11	6 1/2	5.94	8 1/2	7.77
5/8	0.57	2 5/8	2.40	4 5/8	4.23	6 5/8	6.06	8 5/8	7.89
3/4	0.69	2 3/4	2.51	4 3/4	4.34	6 3/4	6.17	8 3/4	8.00
7/8	0.80	2 7/8	2.63	4 7/8	4.46	6 7/8	6.29	8 7/8	8.12
1	0.91	3	2.74	5	4.57	7	6.40	9	8.23
1 1/8	1.03	3 1/8	2.86	5 1/8	4.69	7 1/8	6.52	9 1/8	8.34
1 1/4	1.14	3 1/4	2.97	5 1/4	4.80	7 1/4	6.63	9 1/4	8.46
1 3/8	1.26	3 3/8	3.09	5 3/8	4.91	7 3/8	6.74	9 3/8	8.57
1 1/2	1.37	3 1/2	3.20	5 1/2	5.03	7 1/2	6.86	9 1/2	8.69
1 5/8	1.49	3 5/8	3.31	5 5/8	5.14	7 5/8	6.97	9 5/8	8.80
1 3/4	1.60	3 3/4	3.43	5 3/4	5.26	7 3/4	7.09	9 3/4	8.92
1 7/8	1.71	3 7/4	3.54	5 7/4	5.37	7 7/4	7.20	9 7/4	9.03
2	1.83	4	3.66	6	5.49	8	7.32	10	9.14

Index

Acknowledgements

Many good friends and colleagues have helped me in the preparation of this book, and I would like to acknowledge their assistance and support.

On a professional level, I want to thank my friends and publishers, **Susan and Gareth Jenkins** for their vision and enthusiasm. **Penny Brown** has been a joy to work with; her drawings and paintings are exquisite and have brought the instructions in this book to glorious life. **Colin Mills** has wrought magic with his camera, and has beautifully captured the seasonal glory of the quilts and projects. I was delighted to work with **Carole Thomas** again; her good humour, patience and professionalism as the design director for this book are just as I remembered from our early days of working together. I'd also like to thank the assistant designer, **Gabrielle Markus**, for all her hard work, particularly on sunny summer weekends! Many thanks to **Judy Hammersla** who read the manuscript from a quilter's point of view and made the appropriate corrections. **Fabric traditions** 1350 Broadway #2106, New York, NY 10018 USA, provided many of the fabrics used to construct the small projects in this book. **Betsey Telford** of Rocky Mountain Quilts, 3847 Alt 6 & 24, Palisade, CO 81526, USA loaned the antique fabrics featured on page 9. A special thank you to **Ray Daffurn** who was never too busy to find time to take yet another photograph.

I don't know whether the following people should be thanked on a personal or professional level, because only friends would have done what they did for me on such short notice, yet only professionals could have done it so well. **Monica Millner** made the Oak Leaf and Reel Wall Hanging, the Framed Summer Berries block, the Rose Wreath Centerpiece and she did the appliqué work on the Spring Bouquet Frilly Cushion. **Judy Hammersla** made the Art Deco Fans Placemat and Napkin, the Love Apple Baby Quilt and the Sunflowers Lap Quilt. **Jean Edwards** made the Evergreen Table Runner and the Double Irish Chain Christmas Stocking. **Lisa Benjamin** made the Schoolhouse Tote Bag. **Ann Ryan** made the Cactus Basket Pot Holders.

On a personal level, I would like to thank my *au pair* **Isa Andersson**, who helped me in so many ways I cannot begin to name them; suffice it to say that I couldn't have written this book without her help. **Annlee Landman** has been a source of support, ideas and encouragement – an invaluable friend as always. My daughters, **Alysson and Emily**, have been very understanding of a mother who didn't seem to want to play with them anymore and who was always sitting in front of the computer working when *they* wanted to play with it! Finally, I'd like to thank my husband **Robert** for his advice, understanding and assistance, and for his never-failing sense of subtle humour that keeps me going.